Free Speech: A Very Short Introduction

Very Short Introductions available now:

Nigel Warburton

FREE SPEECH

A Very Short Introduction

OXFORD

UNIVERSITY PRESS

Great Clarendon Street, Oxford OX2 6DP

Oxford University Press is a department of the University of Oxford.
It furthers the University's objective of excellence in research, scholarship,
and education by publishing worldwide in

Oxford New York

Auckland Cape Town Dar es Salaam Hong Kong Karachi
Kuala Lumpur Madrid Melbourne Mexico City Nairobi
New Delhi Shanghai Taipei Toronto

With offices in

Argentina Austria Brazil Chile Czech Republic France Greece
Guatemala Hungary Italy Japan Poland Portugal Singapore
South Korea Switzerland Thailand Turkey Ukraine Vietnam

Oxford is a registered trade mark of Oxford University Press
in the UK and in certain other countries

Published in the United States
by Oxford University Press Inc., New York

British Library Cataloguing in Publication Data

Data available

Library of Congress Cataloging in Publication Data

Data available

ISBN 978–0–19–923235–2

10

Typeset by SPI Publisher Services, Pondicherry, India
Printed in Great Britain by
Ashford Colour Press Ltd, Gosport, Hampshire

Contents

Preface

My aim in this book is simple. I want to provide a critical overview of the main arguments about what free speech is and why we should care about it.

Chapter 1 gives an overview of some of the key debates and recent cases. In Chapter 2 I outline the main features of the classic liberal defence of free speech. In Chapter 3, I explore the issue of causing offence: in particular I look at the suggestion that religious believers should receive special protection against offence. Chapter 4 focuses on pornography and the various arguments for and against censorship; it also includes a discussion of whether works of art should be given special protection from censorship. In Chapter 5 I consider several ways in which the Internet is transforming questions about free speech including through calling into question existing approaches to copyright. In the final short chapter I speculate about the future of free speech.

Michael Clark, Richard Combes, Andrew Copson, Stuart Franklin, Alan Haworth, Heather McCallum, Cathal Morrow, and several anonymous readers all either commented on a draft of this book or suggested relevant examples, for which I am very grateful. I am particularly grateful to David Edmonds and Anna Motz for detailed feedback and discussion of ideas in this book over the past year and for their close reading of various drafts. Thanks too to Luciana O'Flaherty, James Thompson, Keira Dickinson and Andrea Keegan at OUP, and to Deborah Protheroe who researched the illustrations.

List of illustrations

The publisher and the author apologize for any errors or omissions in the
above list. If contacted they will be pleased to rectify these at the earliest
opportunity.

Chapter 1
Free speech

'I despise what you say, but will defend to the death your right to say it.'

This declaration, attributed to Voltaire, encapsulates the idea at the core of this book: freedom of speech is worth defending vigorously even when you hate what is being spoken. Commitment to free speech involves protecting the speech that you don't want to hear as well as the speech that you do. This principle is at the heart of democracy, a basic human right, and its protection is a mark of a civilized and tolerant society.

Article 19 of the United Nations' Universal Declaration of Human Rights and the First Amendment to the US Constitution both explicitly recognize the need to protect free expression.

The First Amendment

> Congress shall make no law ... abridging the freedom of speech, or of the press, or of the people peaceably to assemble, and to petition the Government for a redress of grievances.
>
> **First Amendment to the US Constitution**

> ## Universal Declaration of Human Rights
>
> 'Everyone has the right to freedom of opinion and expression; this right includes freedom to hold opinions without interference and to seek, receive and impart information and ideas through any media and regardless of frontiers.'
>
> Article 19, Universal Declaration of
> Human Rights, UN 1948.

In both cases this indicates the free speech principle's fundamental importance, but it is also an acknowledgement of how fragile this freedom can be if it is not protected. The presumed purpose of the First Amendment was to block central government from making incursions into this area. It is a bulwark against using censorship as if it were a legitimate instrument to prevent criticism of government policy. The temptation to use law or force to gag opponents of one kind or another is difficult to resist. Without freedom to criticize and challenge those acting on our behalf, democracies may degenerate into tyrannies. But it is not just governments that restrict freedom of speech and it is not just political speech that warrants protection.

Though I will discuss a number of legal cases, this is not a book about Human Rights Law or the interpretation of the First Amendment. My aim is to provide a critical overview of the main arguments about free speech, its value and limits. Where I discuss particular laws this is always in the context of a wider philosophical concern about the moral justification for these laws. The basic questions that drive this book are moral: 'What is the value of free speech?' and 'What limits should we set to free speech?' All human beings have an interest in being allowed to express themselves and in having the opportunity to hear, read, and see other people's free expression. Free speech is of particular value within a democratic society.

Belief in the importance of free speech is not an inherited dogma of the Enlightenment, though some have argued that that is all it is. Karl Marx thought that liberal rights tended to preserve the interests of an individualistic bourgeoisie rather than the permanent interests of humanity. I disagree. Declaring a right to extensive free speech is not shorthand for the protection of the speech of those in positions of power, whether economic or political.

Free speech is of particular value in a democratic society. In a democracy voters have an interest in hearing and contesting a wide range of opinions and in having access to facts and interpretations, as well as contrasting views, even when they believe that the expressed views are politically, morally, or personally offensive. These opinions may not always be communicated directly through newspapers and radio and television, but are often presented in novels, poems, films, cartoons, and lyrics. They can also be expressed symbolically by acts such as burning a flag, or as many anti-Vietnam War protestors did, burning a draft card. Members of a democracy also have an interest in a wide range of citizens being active participants in political debate rather than passive recipients of policy delivered from above.

Some have gone further than this and argued that government without extensive freedom of speech would not be legitimate at all and should not be called 'democratic'. On this view democracy entails more than commitment to elections and universal suffrage: extensive protection of free speech is a precondition of any democracy that merits the name, since without it government couldn't be genuinely participatory; this is Ronald Dworkin's position:

> Free speech is a condition of legitimate government. Laws and policies are not legitimate unless they have been adopted through a democratic process, and a process is not democratic if government

has prevented anyone from expressing his convictions about what those laws and policies should be.

If, in a democracy, I have views about how my political representatives are acting, then on this account I should be allowed to express those views in ways that go far beyond putting a cross against a candidate's name on a ballot form every few years.

Yet the situation is far from simple. There are foreseeable and dangerous consequences of many types of expression. There are cases where other factors may be more important than free speech. Where national security is seriously threatened, for example, or where there is a risk of serious harm to children, many people are prepared to restrict freedom of speech to some degree for the sake of other ends. As Tim Scanlon has pointed out, free speech has costs:

> What people can say can cause injury, can disclose private information, can disclose harmful public information. It's not a free zone where you can do anything because nothing matters. Speech matters.

The difficulty here is framing the exceptions to the presumption of free speech in such a way that consistent application of the principle doesn't permit less desirable censorship. There is also a reasonable fear that every act of censorship tolerated makes further censorship easier to achieve; this fear of gradual erosion is one reason why seemingly minor restrictions of liberty can evoke such strong responses in those who value free speech.

What does 'speech' mean?

Throughout this book I will use 'free speech' in a broad way to cover not just the spoken word (the strict meaning of 'speech') but a wide range of expression, including the written word, plays, films, videos, photographs, cartoons, paintings, and so on. In most controversial cases of ideas expressed in speech or writing the context of the expression determines its meaning. The act of expressing the idea in a particular place at a particular time has a foreseeable impact, and listeners and readers understand an expression as having been deliberately delivered in that context with an anticipated interpretation. Similarly the context of presentation of a film, video, photograph, drawing, or painting will directly affect how it is received. To understand any particular example of free speech or free expression requires, then, an appreciation of when the expression was made, to whom, with what intended or at least predictable effect.

As I have already mentioned, ideas can be expressed through symbolic public acts such as destroying a flag or burning a draft card. When such acts are clearly intended to communicate a message, the fact that they don't involve words does not prevent them being examples of speech. If, by law or force, individuals are prevented from communicating their views through such symbolic behaviour their freedom of speech is restricted. The United States Supreme Court ruled in 1969 that wearing black armbands in school was protected as a communicative act covered by the First Amendment.

Free speech is not typically an issue in relation to a private conversation or a soliloquy delivered to a mirror in the bathroom—not unless your room has been bugged, as happened to some suspected dissidents in East Germany during the Cold War. Questions about free speech typically arise in relation to public communication of one sort or another: publishing a book, a poem, an article, or a photograph, broadcasting a radio or television programme, creating and exhibiting a work of art, giving a speech to a political rally, or perhaps posting a diatribe on a weblog or speaking on a podcast. Free speech is especially important for writers of both fiction and non-fiction since the essence of their activity is to communicate ideas in public. For non-fiction writers, freedom to communicate the truth as they understand it is vital; for fiction writers, limits put on the ideas they can express, for ideological, religious, or other reasons, cuts to the heart of their creativity. For more than thirty years the journal *Index on Censorship* has had little difficulty in filling its pages with examples of writers who have been denied this fundamental right of communication. The world's jails house many writers who have in the eyes of their accusers overstepped the acceptable limits on what they communicate, and many of the greatest writers in history have been imprisoned, tortured, or even killed for expressing their ideas.

The term 'free speech' has the merit of connecting with the idea of the individual communicating in one of the most direct and personal ways we have available to us, through the voice. 'Free expression' is in some ways more accurate, but it also carries with it the connotation that what is expressed is somehow subjective; whereas in many controversial cases in which writers and others are censored there is nothing subjective about the facts they are trying to communicate to a wider audience. A Chinese writer who provides details about precisely how many students died in the 1989 massacre in Tiananmen Square, for example, is not so much 'expressing' an idea as communicating facts. If the Chinese government prevents him from speaking, the facts remain.

Censorship is often described metaphorically as a removal of an individual or group's *voice*. When in 1988, the British government wanted to dilute the power of Sinn Fein leaders' message, it is significant that they literally removed their voices by having actors speak their words during news broadcasts. It was thought that the words themselves would be less powerful when spoken in a neutral tone by an actor who, presumably, did not believe in them, rather than by Gerry Adams or Martin McGuinness, the Sinn Fein leaders. This bizarre policy backfired: each news broadcast served as a non-verbal reminder that Sinn Fein leaders were to some degree being denied freedom of speech.

Another aspect of the topic of free speech rarely mentioned is that in a climate where people do not feel able to express their views, or are actively prevented from doing so, it may not be possible simply to internalize the illicit view. Many of us don't know precisely what we think until we try to express ourselves to an audience or at least a potential audience, and most thinkers develop their ideas by interacting with others who agree or disagree with what they think. While it is true that some political prisoners have written poetry in their heads, only an exceptional writer would be able to house a whole novel or a book-length work of non-fiction in their memory. Furthermore, some kinds of writing require extensive research: where a state forbids the expression of certain sorts of ideas, access to the materials needed to express those ideas in convincing form is also typically denied. Solitary confinement is an especially effective means of censorship and widely practised against dissident writers and thinkers. Threat of imprisonment, torture, or death can also curb the kinds of discussion that act as a catalyst for expression. But history has shown that many people are undaunted by such threats and are brave enough to speak even when it will mean certain and painful death.

What does 'free' mean?

The philosopher Isaiah Berlin famously distinguished between two concepts of freedom: negative and positive. Negative freedom is absence of constraint. You are free to do something in this negative sense if nobody is restricting you from doing it. You are free now to stand up if no one is preventing you from doing this. Positive liberty, in contrast, is the freedom actually to achieve what you want to do. You may, for example have internal psychological blocks that prevent you expressing yourself as you wish even though no one is actively preventing you from speaking. In Berlin's terms you would be free in the negative sense, but not the positive.

In this book I focus on the negative sense of freedom. The history of free speech is a history of attempts to prevent people communicating their views whether by censorship, imprisonment, restrictive laws, actual and implicit threats of violence, book burning, search engine blocking or, in the most extreme cases, execution. It is worth noting, however, that some Marxist philosophers, such as Herbert Marcuse in his essay 'Repressive Tolerance', have argued that lack of censorship doesn't guarantee that freedom will be exercised in any worthwhile way. In a society where the general population has been indoctrinated and manipulated by those who control the media, free speech may simply serve the interests of the powerful and be as effective as repressive censorship in a totalitarian society. Whether or not he is accurate about the malleability of the general population, his solution—censorship of 'regressive movements', particularly those on the political right—is a paradoxical form of intolerance in the name of tolerance.

Liberty not licence

Defenders of free speech almost without exception recognize the need for *some* limits to the freedom they advocate. In other words, liberty should not be confused with licence. Complete freedom of speech would permit freedom to slander, freedom to engage in false and highly misleading advertising, freedom to publish sexual material about children, freedom to reveal state secrets, and so on. Alexander Meiklejohn, a thinker who was particularly concerned to nurture the sorts of debate that are fruitful for a democracy made this point:

> When self-governing men demand freedom of speech they are not saying that every individual has an unalienable right to speak whenever, wherever, however he chooses. They do not declare that any man may talk as he pleases, when he pleases, about what he pleases, about whom he pleases, to whom he pleases.

This is important. The kind of freedom of speech worth wanting is freedom to express your views at appropriate times in appropriate places, not freedom to speak at any time that suits you. Nor should it be freedom to express any view whatsoever: there are limits.

John Stuart Mill, the most celebrated contributor to debates about the limits of individual freedom, and the main subject of Chapter 2, despite advocating considerably more personal freedom of expression than most of his contemporaries were comfortable with, set the boundary at the point where speech or writing was an incitement to violence. He was also clear that his arguments for freedom only applied to 'human beings in the maturity of their faculties'. Paternalism—that is, coercing someone *for their own good*—was in his opinion appropriate towards children, and, more controversially, towards 'those backward states of society in which the race itself may be considered in its nonage'. But it was not appropriate towards adult members of a civilized society: they should be free to make their own minds up about how to live. They should also be free to make their own mistakes.

Judge Oliver Wendell Holmes Jr's memorable observation that freedom of speech should not include the freedom to shout 'Fire!' in a crowded theatre captures an important point that is easily ignored when rhetoric about freedom takes over: defenders of free speech need to draw a line somewhere. The emotive connotations of the word 'freedom' should not blinker us to the extent that we forget this. Allowing someone to shout 'fire' in a crowded theatre might cause a stampede resulting in injury or even death, and a hoax might also undermine theatregoers' reactions to a genuine cry of 'fire'. Holmes made his comment in a Supreme Court judgment (*Schenck v United States*) relating to the First Amendment. He gave this judgment in 1919, but the offending act, printing and circulating 15,000 anti-war leaflets to enlisted soldiers during wartime, took place in 1917. The pamphlets declared that the drafting of soldiers was a 'monstrous wrong against humanity in the interest of Wall Street's chosen few'. For Holmes the context of any expression in part determined whether it could justifiably be censored. While this expression of ideas might have had First Amendment protection in peacetime, the same ideas expressed during a war should be treated differently and did not merit that protection. Here the war effort could have been seriously undermined, so Holmes declared these special circumstances justified a special restriction on freedom:

> The question in every case is whether the words used are used in such circumstances and are of such a nature as to create a clear and present danger that they will bring about the substantive evils that Congress has a right to prevent. It is a question of proximity and degree. When a nation is at war many things that might be said in time of peace are such a hindrance to its effort that their utterance will not be endured so long as men fight, and that no court could regard them as protected by any constitutional right.

Holmes, like Mill, was committed to defending freedom of speech in most circumstances, and, explicitly defended the value of a 'free trade in ideas' as part of a search for truth, though unlike Mill he gave a pragmatic account of truth: 'the best test of truth', he maintained, 'is the power of the thought to get itself accepted in the competition of the market'. Holmes wrote passionately about what he called the 'experiment' embedded in the US Constitution arguing that we should be 'eternally vigilant' against any attempt to silence opinions that we despise *unless* they seriously threaten the country—hence the 'clear and present danger' test outlined in the quotation above. Holmes as a judge was specifically concerned with how to interpret the First Amendment; his was an interest in the application of law. Mill in contrast was not writing about legal rights, but about the moral question of whether it was ever right to curtail free speech whether by law, or by what he

1. Oliver Wendell Holmes Jr., a defender of free speech, yet famous for his observation that it didn't include freedom to shout 'Fire!' in a crowded theatre

described as the tyranny of majority opinion, the way in which those with minority views can be sidelined or even silenced by social disapproval.

Both Mill and Holmes, then, saw that there had to be limits to free speech and that other considerations could on occasion defeat any presumption of an absolute right (legal or moral) to freedom of speech. Apart from the special considerations arising in times of war, most legal systems which broadly preserve freedom of speech still restrict free expression where, for example, it is libellous or slanderous, where it would result in state secrets being revealed, where it would jeopardize a fair trial, where it involves a major intrusion into someone's private life without good reason, where it results in copyright infringement (e.g. using someone else's words without permission), and also in cases of misleading advertising. Many countries also set strict limits to the kinds of pornography that may be published or used. These are just a selection of the restrictions on speech and other kinds of expression that are common in nations which subscribe to some kind of free speech principle and whose citizens think of themselves as free.

Where to draw the line?

If, having read this far, you are still tempted to say that free speech should never be restricted under any circumstances, consider an imaginary case suggested by the philosopher Thomas Scanlon. What would you say about a misanthropic inventor who discovers an easy way to make a highly effective nerve gas from readily available domestic products? Surely in that situation it would be right to prevent him handing out the recipe or otherwise broadcasting it. Very few people would want to defend his right to free speech in relation to this dangerous invention, an invention that could have no obvious benefit to humanity and many possible costs. Even if the inventor did not intend his invention to be used in a harmful way, it still would surely be right to prevent this dangerous information being widely circulated. If you believe that free speech should be defended in every circumstance, then you must believe that it should be defended even in cases like this one.

If the case of the nerve gas inventor sounds contrived, consider the real case of the book *Hit Man: A Technical Manual for Independent Contract Killers*. This book, allegedly written as a work of fiction, gave detailed guidelines about how to kill discreetly and dispose of bodies. It was published in 1983 in the United States. It came to wider public attention when Lawrence Horn hired a hit man to murder his son, his ex-wife, and his son's nurse in order to collect an insurance settlement. The hit man had followed to the letter instructions in the book about how to make the gun difficult to trace, using a homemade silencer, shooting at close range, and so on. The hit man was sentenced to death, and Horn was given life imprisonment. A case was brought against the publishers of the book with the publishers mounting a First Amendment defence. The matter was eventually settled by the publishers out of court. For some, attempting to prosecute the publishers of this book was an attack on free speech; for others it was a morally appropriate reaction to prevent the wider circulation of a work that had inspired and provided an instruction manual for murder and might well do again. Many of those who considered censorship in this case an unacceptable limit on free speech found the book irresponsible and dangerous, but were still worried about the risk of curtailing free speech, particularly as much of the information in the book was already very widely available in gangster movies and true crime books. If the book could be shown to be a direct incitement to violence, then there would be clear grounds for censorship; if not, then this looked like an encroachment on individual liberty.

To declare 'I'm in favour of free speech', then, is relatively uninformative without an idea of where the limits lie, and for most people this does not mean 'I'm in favour of free speech in absolutely every circumstance.' But deciding precisely where to draw these limits is no easy task. It means deciding when some competing value has priority over this freedom. In the *Schenk* case, national security in wartime was deemed (retrospectively) of higher value; in the *Hit Man* case there was a genuine concern that publishing this book carried a significant risk of dangerous consequences and had perhaps already inspired a multiple murder.

A slippery slope argument

But perhaps almost any curtailment of freedom of speech should be contested on the grounds that to allow a government to restrict such a basic freedom is to take a step down a slippery slope that will almost inevitably end in totalitarianism. Without a Bill of Rights, the United Kingdom may be vulnerable in this respect when compared with the United States. Indeed, distrust of governments and their ability to censor on reasonable grounds is an important motivation for defending some kind of free speech principle. Yet the presence of a principle such as the First Amendment has its own associated difficulties: like almost any principle, it is open to a wide range of interpretations as the history of First Amendment jurisprudence has demonstrated, with fierce debates about the application and limits on the principle of free expression that this constitutional clause protects.

The benefits of preserving freedom of speech according to the slippery slope argument include protection from descent into a totalitarian regime or at least to something close to it. This approach suggests that we should preserve freedom of speech because of the good consequences that flow from this. The cruder versions of this argument are, however, easily refuted. Slippery slopes may be more or less slippery, and in some cases it is possible to dig one's heels in and say 'Here and no further'. In other words, the fact that a government decides to give national security a higher weighting in some instances than freedom of speech does not mean that this democratic government will inevitably metamorphose into a totalitarian regime. The question here is an empirical one about how likely descent is in such circumstances. Just because we can move from an open democracy to a totalitarian state by a series of small moves, it does not follow that if we take one step away from open democracy we will necessarily end up with totalitarianism. Another way of putting this, continuing the metaphor, is that slopes may be more or less slippery, steeper, and shallower. Further empirical evidence is needed to support the claim of *inevitable* descent into totalitarianism. A second line of criticism is that we are already some way from a society in which total freedom of speech is protected, and yet we do not seem to be hurtling towards totalitarianism.

Nevertheless, this slippery slope argument still does have some weight. In the United Kingdom a new law was imposed in 2005 (Serious Organized Crime and Police Act) forbidding public protest within a kilometre of the Houses of Parliament. One of the first people to be prosecuted under this law, Maya Evans, was guilty of reading out the names of those killed in Iraq since the recent invasion, without police authorization. A Bill of Rights might have made it harder or even impossible for government to have imposed this legislation. It could plausibly be argued that once a one-kilometre exclusion zone has been created, as it has, then extending this to say two or three kilometres, or rolling out similar laws near other potential terrorist targets, will be significantly easier. The slippery slope here may not lead inexorably to totalitarianism, but it could remove important freedoms from those living in the United Kingdom, freedoms which could curb or at least dilute political protest. On this sort of argument one of the great values of having a Constitution is that such incremental laws are far harder to initiate and to extend.

Instrumental and moral arguments for free speech

Broadly, there are two kinds of argument that are used to defend free speech. Instrumental arguments rely on the claim that preserving free speech produces tangible benefits of some kind, whether in terms of increased personal happiness, a flourishing society, or even economic benefits. For example, Alexander Meiklejohn argued that the principal value of free speech is that it promotes the kind of discussion that is essential for democracy to function effectively. In order to make good judgements, citizens need to be exposed to a range of ideas; free speech allows citizens to be informed about a variety of views by people who strongly believe in them. This last point is important, since those playing devil's advocate can rarely imagine themselves into the position of a genuine and passionate believer of the position they are adopting. The ideal is to hear dissenting views from real dissenters not from those imagining what a dissenter might say.

Such arguments appeal to consequences and as such the answer to the question of whether free speech benefits society or individuals in a particular way is an empirical one: there is a right answer, whether or not we know what that answer is, and that answer can in principle be discovered by investigation of probable and actual consequences. The flip side of this approach is that if the supposedly beneficial consequences of free speech can be shown in fact not to follow, then this justification for preserving free speech evaporates.

Moral arguments for free speech typically move from a conception of what it is to be a person, to the idea that it is an infringement of someone's autonomy or dignity—either as a speaker or a listener, or both—to have speech curtailed. It is simply wrong to prevent me speaking my views (or hearing other people's), whether or not good will ensue from what I say, because that would be failure to respect me as an individual capable of thinking and deciding for myself. Such arguments are based on a notion of the intrinsic value of free speech and its connection with a concept of human autonomy rather than any measurable consequences that might flow from preserving it.

Free speech today

The relevance of debates about free speech to contemporary life is obvious. Ever since the invention of the book, people in positions of power have burnt them in symbolic acts of destruction. Girolamo Savonarola's notorious 'Bonfire of the Vanities' of 1497 in Florence was following in a long tradition. The point of that fire was to destroy objects, including immoral books, which might tempt their owners to sin. Variations on that theme persist today.

We live in an age when book burning and censorship are on the rise, and where some acts of expression result in international responses involving many millions of protestors. There are regular calls to curb pornography, hate speech, and Holocaust denial. In some countries extensive state censorship is the norm and there are real risks attached to attempting to express any but orthodox views. The most visible manifestations of intolerance to other people's views and the loudest calls for censorship in recent years, have, though, come from those who feel their religion has in some way been insulted.

The Satanic Verses and the Danish cartoons

In the United Kingdom a pivotal moment was the reaction to the publication of Salman Rushdie's novel *The Satanic Verses* in 1988. It was banned in India and South Africa soon after its publication in the United Kingdom. The novel includes several passages that were considered deeply offensive to Islam by many Muslims. In January 1989, Muslims in Bradford burned copies of the book in a symbolic protest at a rally. Many of them thought Rushdie's novel was deliberately insulting and were outraged by the perceived slur against their religion and their prophet. This resulted in mass rallies of protest both attacking and defending the book. In 1989 the Ayatollah Khomeini declared a *fatwa* against Rushdie—essentially an incitement to kill him. There were acts of courage by publishers, booksellers, and translators in the teeth of threats of violence sanctioned by religious authority. The Japanese translator of the book was killed. Rushdie had to be given police protection and went into hiding for his own safety. Nevertheless, the book is still in print and freely available from bookshops in the United Kingdom and elsewhere.

Whilst Europe has a long history of public burning of books, this was for many a shocking demonstration of intolerance towards written ideas expressed in the form of fiction that almost overnight transformed the way in which freedom of speech was discussed. What had often been an abstract ivory tower debate became a polarized discussion about where the acceptable limits of free speech lie in a democracy that strives to be multicultural.

The debate was reignited by the events of 2005 when the Danish newspaper *Jyllands-Posten* published twelve cartoon images of Muhammad presented as a contribution to debates about self-censorship. One of the most controversial of these depicted Muhammad with a bomb in the shape of a turban on his head. An editorial in the newspaper stressed that having religious groups demand special consideration of their own religious feelings was incompatible with contemporary democracy. Many people, but particularly Muslims, considered these cartoons offensive, blasphemous, and deliberately provocative, not to mention racist. The cartoons were reproduced in newspapers in several European countries, though newspaper editors in Britain decided against printing them. Worldwide protests led to violence, burning of Danish embassies, and a large number of deaths, perhaps as many as a hundred. Some Muslim leaders even issued death threats against the cartoonists.

2. Angry Muslim protestors outside the Danish Embassy in London in February 2006 react to the publication of cartoons of Muhammad in a Danish magazine by attacking freedom of expression itself

In London a demonstration about the cartoons outside the Danish Embassy on 3 February 2006, at which protestors carried banners with exhortations such as 'Liberalism Go To Hell', 'Butcher Those Who Mock Islam', 'Behead Those Who Insult Islam' and even 'Freedom of Expression Go To Hell' and chanted anti-Danish and anti-American slogans, led to arrests and charges of soliciting murder and stirring up racial hatred. Summing up in the charges against Umram Javed, who was found guilty, the Crown Prosecution's Sue Hemming acknowledged the protestors' rights to free speech, but added:

> ... when we examined the content of Mr Javed's speech it was explicit that there was direct encouragement to those present and watching via the media to commit acts of murder against the Danish and Americans.

Free speech surfaced in this controversy in a number of ways. The initial motivation for publishing the cartoons was to assert free speech and emphasize that in a modern democracy it was inappropriate for particular groups to have special protection from offence. The reaction against the cartoons surfaced in some places as an attack on liberalism and the value of free speech. Then, when protestors were prosecuted, some commentators argued that the prosecutions for incitement to murder and racial hatred were a curtailment of free speech and misunderstood the nature of the expressed views: these weren't specific acts of incitement but very generalized expressions of outrage. Underlying the whole affair was the feeling that there was widespread self-censorship by critics of Islam through fear of retaliation.

Yet there is also little doubt that publishing the cartoons was deliberately provocative. Many people felt that this was an immoral taunt with a predictable consequence. The important question here is whether this sort of provocation should be protected by law, rather than restricted by common sense;

whether current law that does protect it is in some way immoral. This is a question which we will return to in Chapter 3.

Religious intolerance of ideas perceived as sacrilegious is by no means restricted to Islam, but the ferocity of opposition to *The Satanic Verses* and to the Danish cartoons has brought questions about free speech into sharp focus. One pressing free speech issue of our day is the question of whether or not a democratic society should heed calls to curb expression that might be thought offensive to religious believers. It is a question that resurfaces in various forms throughout much of this book. But before examining this question, we need to set them in the context of the most influential arguments about the value of free speech, those provided by John Stuart Mill in his short book of 1859, *On Liberty*, a book that has had an effect disproportionate to its length.

Chapter 2
A free market in ideas?

One book continues to dominate philosophical debate about free speech: John Stuart Mill's *On Liberty*. In this classic discussion of the limits of individual freedom in a civilized society Mill defends the view that extensive freedom of speech is a precondition not just for individual happiness, but for a flourishing society. Without free expression humankind may be robbed of ideas that would otherwise have contributed to its development. Preserving freedom of speech maximizes the chance of truth emerging from its collision with error and half-truth. It also reinvigorates the beliefs of those who would otherwise be at risk of holding views as dead dogma.

John Stuart Mill's *On Liberty*

Written against a background of what Mill referred to as the 'tyranny of the majority', the levelling and curbing effect of the opinion of others, *On Liberty* is a passionate defence of the toleration of a wide range of expressions of individuality.

Mill's Harm Principle

Central to Mill's approach throughout *On Liberty* is his 'Harm Principle', the idea that individual adults should be free to do whatever they wish up to the point where they harm another

3. The Victorian philosopher John Stuart Mill, whose *On Liberty* (1859) includes the classic liberal defence of freedom of expression

person in the process. Mill's principle is apparently straightforward: the only justification for interference with someone's freedom to live their life as they choose is if they risk harming other people.

Mill's ultimate defence of this principle was consequentialist—it was based on the belief that by preserving individual freedom, and

> ## Mill's Harm Principle
>
> 'The object of this essay is to assert one very simple principle, as entitled to govern absolutely the dealings of society with the individual in the way of compulsion and control, whether the means used be physical force in the form of legal penalties or the moral coercion of public opinion. That principle is that the sole end for which mankind are warranted individually or collectively, in interfering with the liberty of action of any of their number is self-protection. That the only purpose for which power can be rightfully exercised over any member of a civilized community, against his will, is to prevent harm to others. His own good, either physical or moral, is not a sufficient warrant. He cannot rightfully be compelled to do or forbear because it will be better for him to do so, because it will make him happier, because, in the opinions of others, to do so would be wise or even right.'
>
> From *On Liberty*, chapter 1

tolerating diversity, a society would maximize happiness. In other words, this would produce the best consequences, not least because it provided the conditions under which geniuses best develop. The point of adhering to this principle was that it provided the optimal conditions for human flourishing and progress. Many people would fail to meet their potential if restricted by other people's interventions. Their self-development would be thwarted. This would be bad for all. For Mill, we as human beings are self-directing:

Human nature is not a machine to be built after a model, and set to do exactly the work prescribed for it, but a tree, which requires to grow and develop itself on all sides, according to the tendency of the inward forces which make it a living thing.

24

His ultimate justification for freedom, then, is that it best serves the well-being of each of us and thus all of us. He also believed that other people should not have the deciding say in our development, even if motivated by concern for our own good. We should be free to make our own mistakes rather than be told how we should live. But free speech isn't just another area in which liberal principles apply. For Mill it is a peculiarly important topic because of its relation to truth and human development.

Mill's arguments

In Chapter 2 of *On Liberty*, 'Of the Liberty of Thought and Discussion', Mill sets out several related arguments for protecting freedom of speech, not just from oppressive government intervention, but also from social pressures. Underlying them all are the assumptions that (a) truth is valuable, and (b) no matter how certain someone is that they know the truth, their judgement is still fallible: they might still be wrong. For Mill, a free market of ideas will increase the likelihood of achieving the best result, namely the emergence of truth and the elimination of error. Truth is good for us. Furthermore the process of lively debate with opinions from different sides will reinvigorate views that might otherwise be held in an unthinking way.

Restrictions on free speech will tend to undermine this process, and so produce inferior results. The limit of free speech should be the point at which harm to others is instigated. The benefits to society and to individuals from tolerating extensive freedom of speech, then, are very great; the costs of suppressing it are immense.

Mill is particularly concerned that minority opinions should not be silenced just because they are held by very few people. Unfashionable ideas have potential value for the whole of humanity, even if only held by one person:

> If all mankind minus one were of one opinion, mankind would be
> no more justified in silencing that one person than he, if he had the
> power, would be justified in silencing mankind.

His reason is this. If the view is correct, then humanity
misses the opportunity to exchange truth for error. If, however,
the view is misguided, then we forfeit an opportunity to reinforce
truth through its collision with error. Every opinion has value for
us either because it is true, or else because, though false, it
reinforces the truth and contributes to its emergence.

The infallibility argument

Anyone who silences someone else because they believe the other
person's opinion is false assumes infallibility. They must be
absolutely certain that they are correct on the matter. That is what
Mill suggests. As he points out, however, the psychological state of
certainty in no way guarantees the truth of what we feel certain
about. Individually we make mistakes even about matters we feel
are completely incontrovertible; and collectively whole ages have
made fundamental mistakes about facts—such as whether or not
the Earth orbits the Sun or about the causes of disease and famine.
Galileo was right, but those who silenced him were absolutely
certain that he was wrong.

On another level, many religious believers feel that they
know that a particular god exists. They base their whole lives on
this alleged knowledge. But the different gods of the different
religions can't all exist: many are mutually incompatible.
Monotheism and polytheism, for instance, can't both be true. This
is a point of logic. Nor can the Christian God and the God of the
Muslims both exist; not unless these religions have seriously
misunderstood the nature of their god. Yet Christians and

Muslims may equally have feelings that they genuinely *know* that a particular god exists. On Mill's view they should not assume absolute infallibility because human beings are prone to error about all kinds of beliefs.

Consequently, Mill reasons, it is wrong to assume infallibility in the way a silencer of opinion does. Yet you might think that we have enough certainty on *some* matters not to worry about this objection. Mill's response is that assuming that we possess the truth having gagged or avoided dissenting voices, is very different from holding a view that has been contested openly and emerged unscathed or even strengthened. The process of subjecting a view to critical scrutiny is a necessary part of its validation as certain enough for our purposes.

For Mill freedom to contradict an orthodox opinion is also a condition of intellectual development and of progress. In an atmosphere of intimidation and explicit or implicit danger attached to expressing heretical views, only the brave will speak out. The more timid will have some lines of thought and expression shut off to them, and their mental development will be correspondingly cramped. The claim that authorities are justified in silencing those who express immoral opinions again involves a risky assumption of infallibility that may stunt human progress. Mill cites the cases of Socrates, executed in ancient Athens for alleged impiety, and Christ, in Judaea, executed for what authorities considered immoral teaching. In neither case did the assumed infallibility of the judges stand the test of time. History has judged both Socrates and Jesus worth listening to, their ideas worth discussing.

For Mill, the acknowledgment of his or her own fallibility is part of what makes someone a serious thinker. Human knowledge progresses when people recognize that they may be wrong even on issues that seem certain to them. Wisdom involves openness to those who disagree with us. It is only when our ideas have been subjected to criticism and all objections considered—if necessary seeking these objections out—that we have any right to think of our judgement as better than another's.

The dead dogma argument

Mill makes a powerful case for allowing alleged truths to be challenged. Even if I believe my opinion to be true, and am highly confident about its truth, unless it is 'fully, frequently and fearlessly' discussed, I will end up holding it as a dead dogma, a formulaic and unthinking response. Mill was adamant that our beliefs should not be held as a kind of superstition; rather they should be living truths, truths that their holders could defend when challenged and which might lead to action if appropriate. If you only know your own side of a case, then your belief is likely to be inadequate. You need to be able to refute counter-arguments to your position otherwise you aren't justified in your belief even if it happens to be true.

This is part of Mill's vision of what it is to be human and the importance of thinking through our beliefs so that they are ours and not a mere inheritance from other people. Our beliefs should not be parroted orthodoxies. A belief held out of inclination rather than after due consideration of the arguments both for and against it is of little value to us. Wherever possible we should engage with those who disagree with us, debate and argue with them, hear their side of the issue and understand why they hold the views they do. Mill even recommends playing devil's advocate against your own ideas where there is no actual opponent. Furthermore, where the grounds for believing an opinion aren't regularly challenged, there is, Mill believed, a risk that they will be lost and with them the meaning of the opinion. The result: where there was previously a living belief, there will only be a husk of the meaning. The vital part of the idea will be lost. This would be a loss to humanity.

> ## John Stuart Mill on the value of free speech
>
> 'Were an opinion a personal possession of no value except to
> the owner, if to be obstructed in the enjoyment of it were
> simply a private injury, it would make some difference
> whether the injury was inflicted only on a few persons or on
> many. But the peculiar evil of silencing the expression of an
> opinion is that it is robbing the human race—those who
> dissent from the opinion still more than those who hold it.'

We should, then, according to Mill, strive to preserve a situation
where ideas are vigorously debated from all sides. Otherwise we
risk a kind of mental stagnation that ultimately destroys the
meaning of those ideas. We must avoid the sleepy world of
reassertion, and replace complacency with challenging argument.
Without opponents of our views we will be less alive as thinkers.
And this will be bad not just for us, but for society at large as well.
Progress is achieved through a polite battle of ideas rather than
through one side having exclusive access to the podium. What
Mill desires is the cut and thrust of a good seminar rather than a
monologue. Without the reinvigorating effects of sincere
challenges to our most cherished beliefs we risk becoming lazy
exponents of well-rehearsed positions. As he put it: 'Both teachers
and learners go to sleep at their post as soon as there is no enemy
in the field'. He was surely right about this.

The partly true argument

A further argument Mill used is that there may be elements of
truth within a largely false position. If the position isn't heard,
then the elements of truth may be lost. For example, Mill pointed
out that in the eighteenth century, against a background of
Enlightenment optimism about civilization, science, and progress,
Jean-Jacques Rousseau's view that civilization wasn't necessarily
better than the simple life had an important impact. Mill is
referring here to Rousseau's ideas expressed in his *Discourse on*

Inequality about how within a developed commercial society humanity is frequently corrupted in various ways, an idea that later inspired Karl Marx. It's not that Rousseau was on the whole correct, Mill thinks, but rather that there was a quantum of truth in his position that had been neglected by the blinkered writers who could only see the fruits of progress. The benefit to society of Rousseau's views was that they were *partly* true, and that, by being aired, even with their generally false or exaggerated conclusions, they stimulated later writers to avoiding naive optimism, and have continued to do so long after Rousseau's death.

It doesn't of course follow from Mill's arguments that absolutely every expressive act in every conceivable circumstance should be tolerated (and even encouraged). But he is clear that if listeners or readers are offended by what is said or written, and particularly by the manner in which it is said, this alone should not be a sufficient ground for censorship. As he recognized, anyone who provides a powerful attack on a cherished idea is likely to be perceived as offensive by those who hold that idea, particularly if there is no easy response to refute the challenge. Yet Mill does recognize that in general a certain calmness in the presentation of ideas is desirable.

Where Mill draws a line marking the limits of acceptable free speech is at the point where it becomes an incitement to harm to another person; not psychological harm or economic harm but physical harm. He is explicit that in most cases we should accord speech and other expression of ideas a far greater tolerance than actions, but this too must have limits. When expressing an idea constitutes an act of incitement to 'some mischievous act', then that act of expression is ruled out by his Harm Principle. His famous example here is of the contrast between a newspaper article in which the writer claims that corn dealers are starvers of the poor and the same view spoken (or communicated via a placard) to an angry mob gathered outside a corn dealer's house. The first is a contentious opinion that should be allowed to enter the public debate even if the view is false or immoral; the second is in those circumstances an act of incitement and so is ruled out by the general Harm Principle that Mill defends and applies throughout *On Liberty*. The context of expression determines whether or not it can plausibly be thought to be an incitement to violence. A corn dealer listening to the speaker stirring up the angry mob outside his house would have reason to fear for his life; whereas the same man reading an article in the newspaper over breakfast might disagree strongly, without in any way being endangered by the intemperate expression of a point of view.

Real-life cases are rarely so straightforward. The point at which a strongly voiced opinion shades into incitement to harm is rarely obvious. And many writers would today recognize that psychological harms can be as personally damaging as physical ones, so would be less inclined to focus solely on physical harms than was Mill. This is a topic that we will return to in the next chapter where I discuss Hate Speech. It makes the issue of where to draw the line between acceptable and unacceptable speech far more complicated.

How relevant are Mill's arguments today?

A fundamental objection to Mill's arguments is that they are inappropriately fixated on the truth or falsehood of statements. Mill's model of the arena in which discussions take place is, as we have seen, something like an idealized academic seminar with opinions calmly delivered on each side and truth emerging victorious and invigorated from its collision with error. The point of this extended seminar is to get closer to the truth on any matter and where necessary participants will play devil's advocate to test ideas to their limit. But life isn't a seminar. And truth isn't all that is at stake. Words and other expressions have serious consequences and not everyone uses them in the way that academics discussing a contentious point do (or claim they do).

Mill's vision doesn't capture what typically happens in present-day disputes about free speech.

Holocaust denial

Mill's discussion does, however, shed light on the question of Holocaust denial, and specifically on the pivotal libel trial that the now-discredited historian David Irving brought against the historian Deborah Lipstadt. In a book published in 1994, *Denying the Holocaust*, Lipstadt referred to Irving as 'one of the most dangerous spokespersons for Holocaust denial'.

After publication of the book, Irving sued Lipstadt and her British publisher Penguin UK for libel. In libel law in the United Kingdom the burden of proof lies with the defendant and not the plaintiff.

Deborah Lipstadt on David Irving

The passage that Irving objected to:

'Irving is one of the most dangerous spokespersons for Holocaust denial. Familiar with historical evidence, he bends it until it conforms with his ideological leanings and political agenda. A man who is convinced that Britain's great decline was accelerated by its decision to go to war with Germany, he is most facile at taking accurate information and shaping it to confirm his conclusions. A review of his recent book, *Churchill's War*, which appeared in *New York Review of Books*, accurately analysed his practice of applying a double standard to evidence. He demands "absolute documentary proof" when it comes to proving the Germans guilty, but he relies on highly circumstantial evidence to condemn the Allies. This is an accurate description not only of Irving's tactics, but of those of deniers in general.'

This meant that Lipstadt had to prove that her assessment of Irving as a Holocaust denier was accurate. The process of gathering conclusive evidence against Irving's claims was complex and time consuming. It took several years' research including visits to archives and even to Auschwitz. Eventually Lipstadt's lawyers proved her case in court. She won a convincing victory with the judge declaring that it was 'incontrovertible that Irving qualifies as a Holocaust denier'. He also stated that:

> Irving's treatment of the historical evidence is so perverse and egregious that it is difficult to accept that it is inadvertence on his part.

and

> He has deliberately skewed the evidence to bring it in line with his political beliefs.

This case turned on questions of truth. What was at stake was a question about the facts of history. Was it or was it not true that millions of people were murdered in gas chambers during the Second World War? And was it true that David Irving had deliberately skewed evidence about the Holocaust?

Lipstadt met Irving's Holocaust denial with counter-speech and counter-evidence. Irving in contrast rather than choosing to argue the details with Lipstadt in an academic manner, used the force of law to attempt to silence her. Fortunately Lipstadt and her publisher Penguin were in a position to gather the relevant evidence to contest the libel suit. Many writers and their publishers in that position would have been more or less forced into an out-of-court settlement. There is also the suggestion that some publishers had before the trial been reluctant to publish books critical of Irving for fear that he would also threaten to sue them. Then, in the court of law, the counter-arguments and counter-evidence undermined Irving's claims.

One side-effect of this trial was that historians of the Holocaust went into far greater detail in their evidence against Holocaust deniers than they had done previously. The existence of an enemy in the field was sufficient to focus and reinvigorate their search for more conclusive evidence about precisely how the Nazis set about systematic killing in the Holocaust. Another was to make far better known some of the extreme 'interpretations' Irving has put on the evidence. For example, in her book *History on Trial*, Lipstadt quotes from a 1991 speech Irving gave in Calgary, a speech that was read out in court:

'I don't see any reason to be tasteful about Auschwitz. It's baloney. It's a legend. Once we admit the fact that it was a brutal slave labour camp and large numbers of people did die, as large numbers of innocent people died elsewhere in the war, why believe the rest of the baloney? I say quite tastelessly in fact that more women died on the back seat of Edward Kennedy's car at Chappaquiddick than ever died in a gas chamber in Auschwitz. Oh, you think that is tasteless. How about this. There are so many Auschwitz survivors going around, in fact the number increases as the years go past, which is biologically very odd to say the least, because I am going to form an Association of Auschwitz survivors, survivors of the Holocaust and other liars ... A-S-S-H-O-L-S.'

After the trial Alan Dershowitz wrote:

One reason why false and offensive speech is permitted in most liberal democracies is precisely because the best answer to bad speech is good speech, rather than censorship.

This is essentially one of John Stuart Mill's points about the value of free speech over restriction of speech. In this case Irving, by suing Lipstadt, provided a public forum in which some of his most offensive and misguided speech could be responded to point by point with detailed evidence to back it up and an arbiter in the person of the judge.

The Irving trial has an epilogue that also further illuminates issues of free speech. Austria has laws against the minimization of crimes committed by the Third Reich. In 2006, while visiting Vienna, David Irving was arrested and imprisoned under these laws. From the perspective of the arguments of Mill's *On Liberty*, such rules are damaging to the pursuit of truth. To Mill it was obvious that even false views have a part to play in the free market of ideas. If we silence those who utter falsehoods, we run the risk of becoming dogmatic, of believing without understanding, or feeling passionate about the evidence supporting our beliefs. We also run the risk that such false beliefs will be given greater credence by the very fact that they are suppressed rather than openly refuted. Austria's laws turned Irving into something of a free speech martyr. The London trial where his views were challenged and conclusively refuted in public had far better consequences. Laws preventing specific interpretations of history are clearly antithetical to free speech. But they may also inadvertently glorify those who are silenced by them—hardly the desired effect.

Respect rather than truth

The case of Holocaust denial differs from many contemporary free-speech issues. With Holocaust denial the focus is on fact, on whether specific statements about the past are true or not. Today, though, many conflicts centre on questions of respect and disrespect rather than opinions, truth, and falsehood. So, for example, in 2004 in Birmingham in England, the first production of the play *Behzti* (which means 'dishonour') by the playwright

4. From discredited historian to free speech martyr: David Irving shortly before being imprisoned in Austria

Gurpreet Kaur Bhatti was disrupted by Sikh rioters, who found it offensive. The plot centres on acts of sexual abuse and murder that take place in a *gurdwara*, a Sikh temple. The truth or falsehood of what was portrayed was not the issue. What disturbed the opponents of the play was that it disrespected the sacred nature of the *gurdwara*. This is a common response of religious groups to what they consider blasphemous depictions of their holy figures and places in novels, plays, and cinema. It is not a question of truth, but of whether there should be topics and places that are out of bounds for writers on the grounds that religious (and other) groups will find inappropriate treatment of such topics deeply offensive.

Mill would presumably have defended the performance of the play on the grounds that it expresses views that might be for the benefit of humanity and that it would be wrong to prejudge this. Furthermore, the indirect censorship of the play significantly restricts the playwright's ability to follow her chosen path in life, despite not directly harming others. But Mill's general stance on free speech is insensitive to the precise point at issue here, which is the alleged sanctity of certain symbols, a recurrent theme in religiously motivated attempts to prevent expression that disrespects this.

A further ground for censorship in some regimes may be that the viewpoint censored is actually true. This is not something that Mill considers in *On Liberty*. False views might be relatively harmless to a powerful government, but if, for example, knowledge of how the anti-corruption (and pro-democracy) protestors in Tiananmen Square in 1989 were slaughtered or incarcerated became widespread throughout China, this might be a trigger for political uprising. This might well be the justification for Chinese authorities censoring, with the aid of some Western Internet Service Providers (ISPs), what appears on Internet search engines in China. In other words, Mill's argument that censors assume infallibility may be beside the point here. What the censors in this case are presumably doing is preventing large numbers of people from learning the truth of the matter, not censoring a view which they sincerely believe to be false. It is the truth (or even an approximation of the truth) that is considered dangerous in this context.

5. Tiananmen Square, 1989: a brave student protests against government corruption shortly before the Chinese army open fire on protestors, killing many of them. Through censorship of the Internet and other media many Chinese today are still unaware of what took place and how their government responded

More generally, once we move away from Mill's implicit assumption that all forms of expression assert facts that may be true or false, then the limitations of his approach become even clearer. Debates about censoring pornographic images, for example, the subject of a later chapter, are not typically debates about the truth or falsehood of what is depicted. Hardcore video pornography aspires to accurate representation of the acts performed in front of the camera. The 'cumshot', where a man visibly ejaculates, is a mark of authentic arousal here. It dispels the suspicion that the actors are engaged in a series of choreographed movements while remaining unaffected by the actions they are performing. It exploits photography's documentary potential to connote truth, to denote facts. It is hard to see how Mill's arguments could be transposed here, unless we take pornography to be asserting a general position about, for example, the availability of women (or men) for sex or, as some feminists have argued, that it wrongly gives the message that all women desire sexual subjugation and directly encourages crimes such as rape. In such a case the general assertion is delivered via a specific instance, the part standing for the whole.

'No Platform' Arguments

It might seem to follow from Mill's views about free speech and the value of falsehoods sincerely expressed that we should actively strive to provide a platform for those with whom we strongly disagree. This is a public way of subjecting our views to the toughest test, the collision with sincerely held error. Whether or not inspired by Mill, some people have argued along these lines. For instance, in a debate in 2007 on the topic of free speech at the Oxford Union Society, the President of the Union, Luke Tryl, justified his invitations to Nick Griffin (of the British National Party) and David Irving by claiming that for a proper debate it was important to hear all views, even if they were obnoxious.

Many people believe there are strong arguments for *not* giving such speakers a platform. This might literally be a platform, as in the invitation to the Oxford Union Society, or it might be a metaphorical platform, such as being given space in a reputable newspaper or interviewed about their views for a radio or television programme. Those who take the 'No Platform' stance (e.g. in the form 'no platform for racists' or 'no platform for Holocaust deniers') argue that it is morally wrong for anyone to give such people credibility by allowing them access to these channels of communication, channels that often come with an implied stamp of respectability. For instance, by inviting Irving to speak at the Union Society this might be seen to be endorsing his credentials as an academic historian, and so might lead him to be taken more seriously than he should be.

On the other hand, those who invited Irving stressed that the Oxford Union has a long history of inviting controversial speakers, including, in the past, Malcolm X, and that an invitation to that particular platform carried with it no endorsement of the views of the speaker whatsoever. Speakers are often selected on grounds of notoriety rather than on the likelihood of an intellectual contribution to an important debate.

Similarly, at a zoology conference, the organizing committee might well decide that it would be inappropriate to allow a Young Earth Creationist, someone who takes the Bible as a literal account of the origin of life, to speak from a platform alongside reputable scientists, because this would seem to imply that the Young Earth Creationist's views were scientifically respectable, which they clearly are not. Richard Dawkins cites a wry comment from a scientific colleague on this topic. Whenever a creationist invites him to a formal debate about the evidence for evolution, this scientist replies, 'That would look great on your CV; not so good on mine.'

A variant of the 'No Platform' view is adopted by Deborah Lipstadt, who despite being one of very few people adequately equipped to refute Irving's views on the Holocaust point by point and in great detail, has declined to appear in debate with Irving on the grounds that even to appear with him in public gives him a credibility that he does not deserve. In this case, Lipstadt's appearance as an academic of sound integrity alongside Irving would be tantamount to an indirect endorsement of his respectability as a historian. The point is that as he has been shown to be systematically deceptive about some of his primary sources, he has entirely discredited himself. Any engagement with him could be read as part of his rehabilitation as a researcher.

It is important to distinguish No Platform Arguments from other related phenomena. First, No Platform Arguments are not complete censorship. I can believe in your legal right to air your views without having any obligation to provide you with the means to air them. Particularly in the age of the Internet, most of us can find ways to express our views to a wide audience. Complete censorship is an attempt to prevent all expression of particular views. No Platform Arguments are about avoiding indirectly endorsing a speaker by providing them with a podium from which to deliver their views.

No Platform Arguments should also be distinguished from the view that only the tolerant merit tolerance, that we have no obligation to preserve the freedom of speech of those who would restrict others' speech. This sort of reasoning, tempting as it is, does not merit the label 'free speech'. It may lead to a kind of censorship. Certainly Mill's arguments for free speech will not single out the intolerant as unworthy of being heard. Intolerant people may very well speak the truth on many issues, or their views may contain elements of truth. No Platform Arguments are arguments about what we are doing indirectly by giving certain people a platform, not an absolute refusal to give a platform anywhere as a punishment for the speaker's intolerance.

Mill's pronouncements on free speech might seem to justify inviting extremists to take part in public debates even if you find their views disgusting. Yet Mill as a consequentialist would also have been sensitive to the side effects of such invitations, which in some cases can be very far reaching. He would also very clearly draw a line where speakers' expression amounted to incitement to violence.

Yet where someone is repeatedly prevented from using the press and television to present a message to a wider audience, it might start to seem like informal censorship. If the consequence is that that person's ideas don't get expressed openly and are not subjected to critical scrutiny, then this would be an unfortunate result.

Chapter 3
Giving and taking offence

A repeated refrain in recent years has been that free speech is only truly free speech if it is used responsibly. Some writers claim that an act of giving offence should not be protected by any free speech principle. In other words, when someone sets out to offend an individual or a group (or even does so inadvertently), they should not try to hide behind the shield of free speech. They should be polite and respect other people's sensitivities. To critics this view is simply a denial of any principle of free speech. The point of a free speech principle is that it protects a wide range of types of expression, a far wider range of views than any reasonable person would want to endorse. This means protecting free speech for those whose views we find deeply offensive, irritating, and with whom we strongly disagree. Free speech is for bigots as well as for polite liberal intellectuals. It is not clear why a principle would merit the name 'free speech' if it only protected the views of those we find sympathetic.

Furthermore, to engage in self-censorship to prevent offence would be to succumb to what is sometimes termed 'the heckler's veto', the notion that if someone in your potential audience is likely to be offended by what you say you should not be permitted to speak, or at the very least you should have the decency not to. How plausible is this idea?

As we have seen, John Stuart Mill was explicit that incitement to violence was the point at which intervention to curb free speech was appropriate. Mere offensiveness wasn't sufficient grounds for intervention and should not be prevented by law, by threats, or by social pressure. He recognized that offensive speech can have far-reaching effects. People may seethe with outrage on hearing some views expressed about matters they hold dear. And the source of such outrage is often religion. In an analogous example Mill uses, he questions whether in a predominantly Muslim country the religious majority, who are revolted by the knowledge that some people eat pork, might be justified in preventing non-Muslims from eating pork. His answer is that inasmuch as eating pork is a self-regarding activity that does no direct harm to anyone else (though some may see it as a harm to the pig), it is not the business of the state to interfere, nor should individuals be prevented from making this sort of dietary choice by social pressure or implied or actual threats from a majority. Clearly eating pork is not here an example of speech or obviously of expression, and Mill only discusses pork eating in private. But what would Mill's views be about, for instance, an individual's freedom to write pro-pork-eating articles in a newspaper on sale in such a country? I think it is obvious that he would defend the individual's freedom to express such views, despite their offensive nature for many readers, for the sorts of reasons given in the previous chapter.

Blasphemy

In England and Wales blasphemy against Christianity (but, inconsistently, not towards other religions) was officially a common law offence when I began writing this book. The common law offence was only abolished in June 2008. In fact the law was even more specific than protecting Christianity: it only applied to the established Church, the Church of England. It would not in law have been blasphemy to make defamatory remarks about, say, some aspect of Baptists' belief unless that particular belief was shared by Anglicans. A consequence of this law was that a Muslim could have been prosecuted for making disparaging comments about objects or ideas sacred to the Church of England, but a member of the Church of England would have been free before the law to make similarly disparaging remarks about objects or ideas sacred to Islam. This asymmetry led to arguments that the existing blasphemy laws should be extended so that they no longer discriminated against adherents of particular religions. This would have further restricted freedom of speech to a considerable degree but it would have had the merit of consistency at a high cost to freedom of speech.

Most defenders of free speech see all blasphemy laws as a historical relic of an earlier age and not particularly relevant to a largely secular society. Present-day advocates of a prohibition on blasphemy argue that because religion is the focus of what is most profoundly important for an individual, it should have special protection against verbal abuse of any kind. The situation in Britain was complicated by the constitutional role occupied by the Church of England. The point of anti-blasphemy legislation is to protect people from having the views they hold most dear challenged in a way that they perceive as offensive. Furthermore, some defenders of such laws believe, the law serves the practical purpose of preventing activities that would tend to destroy the fabric of society.

One of the few successful cases of a conviction under blasphemy laws in the United Kingdom in the last fifty years was brought in 1977 by the campaigner Mary Whitehouse against Denis Lemon, editor of the magazine *Gay News*, for publishing a poem, 'The Love that Dares to Speak its Name', by James Kirkup. In this poem a Roman centurion fellates the recently crucified Jesus Christ, ejaculates into his wounds, and is finally penetrated by the risen Christ. The persona of the Centurion also suggests that Christ has previously had sex with all twelve of the apostles. The poem was essentially a homoerotic fantasy and was published in a magazine specifically targeted at gay readers. Whitehouse's argument was that to portray Christ in this way was so deeply offensive to Christians that the full force of the law should be brought against it. The poem was 'a blasphemous libel' and vilified Christ. The courts sentenced Lemon to nine months' suspended sentence and a £500 fine, and *Gay News*'s publisher was fined a further £1,000; a judgment upheld on appeal by the House of Lords. This was a case of legal prohibition on a piece of writing specifically because of its offensiveness to a particular group who had special protection in law. Despite this ruling, a defiant open public reading of the poem in 2002 in London by humanists, including George Melly and Peter Tatchell, was not prosecuted. Peter Tatchell wrote at the time:

> Why should the Christian religion be given privileged protection against criticism and dissent? No other institution enjoys such sweeping powers to suppress the expression of opinions and ideas. In the name of free speech, the right to protest and artistic freedom, the offence of blasphemy should be abolished.

Tatchell's wish has now been granted.

Any blasphemy law potentially contravenes the European Convention on Human Rights. Article 10 of the Convention states, 'Everyone has the right to free expression.' This is a qualified right and may be overridden by decisions taken in the interest of such matters as national security, prevention of disorder or crime, protection of an individual's reputation, and similar considerations. Yet Article 10 has to be balanced with Article 9, which states, 'Everyone has the right to freedom of thought, conscience and religion.' What these Articles embody is the recognition that freedom to express oneself and freedom to choose and engage in one's religion without interference from others (and that includes, explicitly, the freedom to change one's religion) are important values in contemporary European society. For believers the sorts of expression that are likely to be prosecuted under a blasphemy law are the sorts that they believe curb their freedom to pursue a religion (or strongly held belief) without interference. On the other hand, any threat of possible prosecution for anti-religious pronouncements will be perceived as a significant restriction on free expression, and the more religions protected against such expression, the greater the restriction. The difficulty is assessing how much weight to give to each of the considerations captured in Articles 9 and 10 in particular cases. The values of freedom of religion and belief and the value of freedom of speech can come into conflict. There is no straightforward resolution possible without giving one priority over the other. Furthermore, it is not just the remote possibility of a successful prosecution under blasphemy laws that concerns many people, but rather the way in which the existence of such a law can encourage publishers and producers to self-censor.

The underlying question is whether or not a blasphemy law has any rational underpinning, particularly in any society that is composed of people with a wide variety of religious and non-religious outlooks. The immediate difficulty with broadening a historically specific law that only protects one Christian Church from such offence (and so is essentially discriminatory), such as the recently abolished common law offence in England and Wales, is that were it to be broadened to protect all other religions it would be totally unenforceable. The range of sacrosanct topics and figures for Christianity is large, but not so large as the range for Christianity plus Islam plus Judaism plus Hinduism. Many other religions too would need to be included in this list. Once we have got this far, we have the further issue that, out of fairness, humanists, who are non-religious, should have their most central and dearly held beliefs protected too, or else some clear reason why they are treated differently needs to be stated. And what of the difficulty that a monotheist might be offended every time a polytheist mentioned multiple gods and vice versa? Religious, quasi-religious, and many non-religious groups each have a range of sacred objects, places, people, myths, and ideas they cherish. To protect all of these from blasphemous mention would be absurd to try and impossible to achieve.

A counter-argument to this is that the blasphemy law only protected against intemperate or offensive ways of expressing views hostile to the Christian religion, and that this approach could easily be extended to cover other religions too in other places. This was the essence of a law that Tony Blair proposed in 2005 that forbade 'incitement to religious hatred'. This would have had the virtue of treating different religions equally. However, there are some things that if uttered in the most temperate language will still inflame *some* religious fundamentalists and be considered blasphemous or an incitement to religious hatred. And much religious expression is deeply offensive to some non-believers as Richard Dawkins has made clear in his book *The God Delusion*, where he paints a depressing picture of the damage to humanity caused by religion. It is not at all clear why only those with religious beliefs should have their views protected from offence.

The decision of what might count as 'temperate' language is a subtle one. Much of what religious believers have found most offensive in recent years has appeared in the form of parody and humour. To liberal secularists religious believers' persecution of plays, novels, and films may seem like an absence of a sense of humour as well as an unacceptable intervention in adults' freedom to enjoy the entertainment of their choice just so long as no one was harmed in making it and it can't be construed as an incitement to violence. For example, the Monty Python film *The Life of Brian*, which was released in 1979, drew the ire of many Christians. Although the messiah in the film is called Brian, not

6. In the Monty Python team's controversial parody of the life of Jesus, *Life of Brian*, Brian's mother utters the words 'He's not the messiah, he's a very naughty boy'. For some this is sacrilege, for others a good joke.

Jesus, like Jesus he is crucified (he dies singing 'Always look on the bright side of life').

More recently, the surreal musical *Jerry Springer: The Opera* not only parodied reality television, but also Christianity. Like Kirkup's poem, the suggestion that Christ might be homosexual brought many complaints and when a version was shown on television in the United Kingdom on Channel 4, there was even an attempt to use blasphemy laws against its producers. Some Christians disliked the conceit of God, Jesus, the Virgin Mary, and the Devil appearing on a spoof reality television show; others found it inoffensive and funny. An indirect effect of Christian groups' campaigns against the show, however, was to make it almost impossible for it to be performed because of the threat of

7. Blasphemous parody? *Jerry Springer: The Opera* drew the ire of some Christians because of its portrayal of Christ as having homosexual tendencies

disruption. This has widely been perceived as a kind of indirect censorship, an example of the heckler's veto.

One of the musical's creators, the comedian Stewart Lee, has made an interesting point about the rich resources that religious stories and characters provide for a creative artist:

> Believers say religious stories survive because they are literally true, but even rationalists accept that religious tales, myths and folk-stories, while not always actually true, can be true in terms of what they tell us about human experience.

To non-believers it is not obvious why religious accounts, such as the Gospel stories, should have special protection from reuse in a variety of ways since they are, at the very least, a rich cultural source embodying deep psychological truths. Secular heroes, such as Bertrand Russell, have not been immune from parody, by Monty Python and others, why then should religious figures be immune?

The idea that religious beliefs but not others should receive special protection is bizarre: all types of belief should be open to scrutiny, criticism, parody, and potentially ridicule in a free society. Indeed, some views cry out for ridicule and we would be immoral to treat them seriously. The comedian Rowan Atkinson made this point when opposing the United Kingdom's suggested Religious Hatred Bill:

> What is wrong with encouraging intense dislike of a religion? Why shouldn't you do so, if the beliefs of that religion or the activities perpetrated in its name deserve to be intensely disliked? What if the teachings or beliefs of the religion are so outmoded, hypocritical or abusive of human rights that not expressing criticism of them would be perverse?

Some defenders of free speech argue that it is not just temperate expressions of views that should be protected. The idea that freedom of speech should be restricted to reasoned debate in seminar-like conditions, or well-argued newspaper columns, may not capture the spirit of the value that many people want to preserve when they protect the limits of free speech. It also does not do justice to the history of freedom of speech and the once scandalous and persecuted works and acts of expression that have subsequently entered the canon. The novelist Philip Hensher, for example, has argued that freedom of speech should include the freedom not only to criticize government policy in the newspapers, and discuss our beliefs, sexuality, and race openly and frankly without any fear of intimidation, but also to be free 'to shout rude things at a visiting dictator riding down the Mall in the Queen's landau'. Free speech, he maintains, should include freedom to satirize and mock religion. He points out that 'The progress of free speech has been advanced over the centuries, not just by calm, rational argument, but by excess and irresponsibility'.

Oliver Kamm has made a similar point:

> The notion that free speech, while important, needs to be held in balance with the avoidance of offence is question-begging, because it assumes that offence is something to be avoided. Free speech does indeed cause hurt—but there is nothing wrong in this. Knowledge advances through the destruction of bad ideas. Mockery and derision are among the most powerful tools in the process.

Richard Posner has also stressed the important role that offensiveness can play in the market in ideas:

> People get upset when their way of life is challenged, yet that upset may be the beginning of doubt and lead eventually to change. Think of all the currently conventional ideas and opinions that were deeply offensive when first voiced. Perhaps, therefore, a condition of

being allowed to hear and utter ideas that may challenge *other* people's values and beliefs should be the willingness to extend the same right to others and thus agree that offensiveness will not be a permissible ground for punishing expression.

But perhaps the main justification for prohibiting offence against religious beliefs is to prevent *deliberate* offensiveness for its own sake. There are people who delight in offending religious believers. The argument is that *deliberate* attacks on what believers hold most dear should be forbidden. This is because deliberate offence is not conducive to good social relations. If a particular group is regularly the target of deliberately offensive parody (as for example Scientologists are) then it makes it difficult for them ever to be taken seriously, the argument goes. Accidental offence is not the issue since a reasonable person would make amends when he or she discovered that offence had been taken. So, for example, a cartoonist who produced a cartoon of Muhammad, but who had no idea that Islam prohibits the representation of its prophet, would be in a different category from one who set out to stir up defenders of Islam by producing a caricature of Muhammad *because* she knew that Islam had this prohibition which she considered ridiculous and wanted to make this point visually.

One difficulty of this approach is that writers, speakers, cartoonists, film-makers, and other communicators produce works for a wide range of reasons, some of them less clearly defined than others, some overlapping. Rarely is there a single motive and even where there is, in an artistic context, a work is likely to be subject to a range of interpretations. So, for example, Aayan Hirsan Ali's film made in 2004 with Theo van Gogh, *Submission Part One*, depicted verses of the Qur'ān written on a woman's body to make a point about how she believed Islamic teaching can be and has been used to justify immoral treatment of women: one is flogged for committing adultery, another forced to marry a man she loathes, a third beaten by her husband, a fourth abandoned by her father when he learns that his brother raped her. The film was shown on Dutch television. Her intention was not to attack Islam, but to attack what she saw as a failing of Islamic teaching that did not allow adaptation to modern circumstances:

My message was that the Quran is an act of man, not of God. We should be free to interpret it; we should be permitted to apply it to the modern era in a different way, instead of performing painful contortions to try to recreate the circumstances of a horrible past. My intention was to liberate Muslim minds so that Muslim women—and Muslim men, too—might be freer.

This is a radical message within orthodox Islam. Some Muslim leaders thought it an act of sacrilege and a deliberate provocation and denounced it. From Ali's point of view, however, this was not her intention in the film; she was explicit about this in the original text of the script she took to Theo van Gogh, where she wrote: 'I did not write this script to provoke anyone'. In a response to those who criticized her film, she responded that it was a plea for self-reflection within Islam, and that every form of self-expression should be allowed—except for physical and verbal abuse—in the pursuit of this self-reflection. Her aim was not to turn Muslims into atheists, but 'to expose the blemishes of the culture, particularly in its cruel treatment of women'. She knew her film would be controversial. In making the film, however, she was acting well within the law in a country with a long history of protecting and valuing free expression.

In November 2004, Theo van Gogh, the film's director, was shot and killed as he cycled down a street in Amsterdam. His murderer, Muhammed Bouyeri, pinned a five-page letter quoting the Qur'ān and threatening Ali to his chest. Ali was forced to go in to hiding for her own self-protection.

Are we to treat Ali's assertion that she had no intention to provoke anyone as merely disingenuous? It is not clear how it would be possible to adjudicate this sort of case. It bears many similarities to the Islamic reaction to Salman Rushdie's novel *The Satanic Verses*, a reaction that symbolizes an impasse between those who believe in individuals' freedom of expression on matters of religion and many other issues as a non-negotiable aspect of civilized democratic society, and those who insist that their religion should be held sacrosanct, that no one should be permitted to express anything that is in their view blasphemous.

Christianity and Islam are not the only religions capable of intolerance towards criticism or what their adherents perceive as sacrilege. As I mentioned in Chapter 2, in 2004 Sikh protests against Gurpreet Kaur Bhatti's play *Behzti* culminated in a crowd of over a thousand people storming the Birmingham Repertory theatre and three police officers being injured. The playwright had to go into hiding for her own safety. Like Aayan Hirsi Ali, Bhatti was explicit that she was not deliberately offensive in her work:

> I did not write *Behtzi* to offend. It is a sincere piece of work in which I wanted to explore how human frailties can lead people into a prison of hypocrisy.

Nevertheless, the simple outline of the plot was sufficient to offend many of the protestors, few of whom had seen the play. The effects of the storming of the theatre are far wider than the particular case: the danger of such episodes is that they cause writers to self-censor for fear of violence.

The suggestion that creative artists and others should tiptoe around the wide-ranging religious sensitivities of Christians, Muslims, Sikhs, and others, and that religious beliefs should be held as sacrosanct and immune from criticism is unacceptable in an open democracy. A spirit of toleration should not include a prohibition on causing offence. The intolerance shown by some religious believers is deeply offensive to many non-religious people (as well as to some religious believers), but that is not a reason for the non-religious and anti-religious to threaten violence against the intolerant. It is an opportunity to meet speech with counter-speech.

Hate speech

The question of deliberate provocation is important too in justifying laws against what has come to be known as hate speech. Hate speech is expression that aims to cause extreme offence and to vilify its target audience. This is speech or writing, or other expression that is so insulting that it is tantamount to a form of harm (though stopping short of direct incitement to violence), and so, many people believe, should not be immune from censorship in the way that other less offensive expressions should be. In other words, hate speech is often presented as a special category which does not merit free speech protection in the way that other speech does. Some blasphemy might easily be re-described as hate speech directed at the religious, though some is simply a matter of failing to recognize or give special treatment to symbols that others hold dear or sacred.

Hate speech typically degrades people on the basis of their race, religion, or sexual orientation. The choice of language or other form of expression and the context in which it is uttered or written are all organized to achieve insult and humiliation of a group or individual. It is an expression of contempt that gets its effect from hitting the mark: the target group needs to hear, read, or otherwise be aware of the message for it to fulfil the speaker's or writer's intentions. This is not a matter of private expression of loathsome views, but rather of acts of extreme insult provocatively delivered.

Often the hate speech is intended to be contagious—part of the desired effect is to encourage others to express similarly venomous views. Here anyone who wants to defend extensive freedom of expression is faced with a stark choice between the values of freedom and the costs of allowing extreme expressions of racism and homophobia that may threaten individuals' dignity and be so offensive as to interfere with their lives on a daily basis and at a significant level. The targets of hate speech are often particularly vulnerable and in a minority. The cost for them of freedom of speech would be potentially high in that their dignity and self-respect may be threatened.

The extreme liberal position is to defend hate speech as an unfortunate possibility once you have adopted a free speech policy. A full range of sorts of speech merits preservation from prosecution. In the United States, the First Amendment free speech protection has in some renowned cases led to judgments that, disgusting as such hate speech may be, it should still in many cases be permitted. It is protected from prosecution because it is potentially part of a political debate.

Skokie and toleration

Perhaps the most famous such case in the USA, and one that has become synonymous with the idea that free speech involves protection of the speech you hate, occurred in 1977 when a First Amendment defence was used to protect a planned neo-Nazi march through a village, Skokie in Illinois. This village was occupied by many Jewish refugees from Nazism—approximately one in six inhabitants were either Holocaust survivors or related to Holocaust survivors. The marchers were to wear their uniforms and carry swastikas in a parade that would undoubtedly cause great anguish to those whose friends and relatives had been murdered in Nazi concentration camps. The local village board, anticipating the march, had banned parades in military uniforms and required that a $350,000 indemnity bond be paid in advance of any march. Controversially, the American Civil Liberties Union took up the case as a free speech issue (losing many members in the process); as a result the Court of Appeals declared the Skokie council measures unconstitutional because they contravened the First Amendment. The march, however, didn't take place in Skokie, but was moved to a park in nearby Chicago. Since then, despite the distasteful nature of the march, many free speech activists have taken Skokie to be a symbol of what a commitment to free speech should mean in practice, namely extreme toleration.

The rationale for such toleration is at least twofold: first, many believe that the best way to combat hate speech is with further speech: counter-speech as it is often called. Preventing others expressing extreme opinions has long-term consequences for society, and their frustrations may find expression in other even less desirable ways. In the tradition of John Stuart Mill, the line at which hate speech should be illegal is when it becomes an incitement to violence or a clear case of libel. Secondly, the danger of a legal prohibition on some forms of speech is that it makes further prohibitions that much easier, and that, gradually, individuals will be likely to have their freedom of expression limited to a greater and greater degree. Outlawing hate speech may be the thin end of the wedge.

In the United Kingdom, the legal stance is that there are justifiable limits to freedom of speech in relation to hate speech, particularly when others' lives may be blighted by some kinds of expression, and that it is for the courts to draw the line between acceptable and unacceptable forms of expression, taking account of a wide range of factors, difficult as this may be. Laws against racial discrimination, for example, can be used to prosecute those who use racist hate speech. In many other countries too, including Austria, Germany, France, Canada, and New Zealand, there are laws protecting racial groups from certain sorts of targeted expressions of hatred.

Some philosophers, such as Jennifer Hornsby, have argued against the extreme liberal position of the kind demonstrated in the Skokie decision on the grounds that it misconstrues the nature of communication involved. She believes that extreme liberals end up protecting the freedom of those who are least in need of protection; while others are damaged as communicators by hate speech. For liberals, though, that is just part of the heavy cost of preserving free speech; but free speech brings greater overall rewards than censorship. As Kenan Malik has put it

> Free-speech for everyone but bigots is no free speech at all. The right to transgress against liberal orthodoxy is as important as the right to blaspheme against religious dogma or the right to challenge reactionary traditions.

And, as Malik goes on to point out, challenging bigotry by banning it can produce worse results than toleration and counter-speech: 'You simply let the sentiments fester underground.'

Chapter 4
Censoring pornography

Pornography presents a difficult challenge for anyone who believes in freedom of expression. Should pornography be tolerated, in all its manifestations, provided that no one is directly harmed in its making; or are there more important values at stake here than freedom?

Since the invention of the printing press, pornography has been reproduced and circulated widely, though obviously it pre-dated this means of mechanical reproduction. The invention of photography and intrinsically reproducible images that could be rapidly created and which had the added frisson of an implied veracity and fine-grained detail transformed the pornography industry and made some people very rich. Moving images, video, and now digital images combined with global distribution initially via DVDs and cable television and more recently via the Internet, whether downloaded or streamed, have led to an increased availability of pornography combined with greater privacy about its purchase and use. The advent of the digital camera has also democratized the production of pornography: the simplicity of producing high-quality digital images whether still or moving and distributing them on the Internet has meant that many more pornographic images and videos are in circulation than ever before, with many more people accessing them.

What is pornography?

Pornography is predominantly a kind of image making designed to arouse the viewer sexually by representing explicit sexual action of some kind, though not all pornography is visual. There is also audio pornography, which may now take the form of a podcast, and written pornography, which may now be delivered via a weblog or an Internet download rather than printed. Many writers in this area distinguish between hardcore pornography that is particularly explicit, and softcore pornography which sets milder limits on what it depicts.

> **One controversial definition of pornography**
>
> In 1983 Catherine MacKinnon and Andrea Dworkin argued that pornography should be actionable as a violation of civil rights. They gave a non-neutral definition of pornography as: 'the graphic sexually explicit sub-ordination of women through pictures and/or words'.
>
> They went on to list the sorts of content that made a work pornographic, including women being presented as dehumanized, as sexual objects, as commodities, as reduced to body parts, as enjoying being humiliated or hurt, as being shown in degrading situations, and so on. They also allowed that men, children, and transsexuals could equally be victims of pornography in the above sense.

Is hardcore pornography speech?

If hardcore pornography isn't speech in any important sense, it shouldn't have free speech protection. It would then be in a different category from the types of communication that merit special preservation. Political speech and artistic expression communicate ideas that can benefit society even when they are false. Photographic images of sexual acts aren't obviously communicative at all. They are usually close-ups of real and simulated sexual action, with a blurring of the question of whether the stars of the film are acting parts or simply being filmed having sex. Hardcore pornography is usually devoid of emotional content, does not embody thoughts about what it shows, and aspires to transparency to the actions it reveals. It is primarily an aid to sexual arousal. Most of those who enjoy pornography enjoy it for precisely this reason: it is particularly effective at arousing viewers and is standardly a stimulus for masturbation. On this account watching a hardcore pornographic film is in many respects morally akin to peeping through a keyhole and becoming aroused, possibly to the point of orgasm, by seeing people engaged in some kind of scripted sexual activity, albeit with the implied consent of those viewed. The person who provides the keyhole and stages the activity for you is not expressing thoughts, but rather providing you with a way of seeing something you might not otherwise have seen. It is more like someone pointing something out to you.

This view of what photographic pornography is could gain support from Kendall Walton's account of the nature of photography. He has argued that photographic realism is different from realism in other forms of picture making. According to him, photographs literally allow us to see through them to what was in front of the lens in a non-metaphorical sense of 'see'. A photograph of sexual activity, on this view, allows us to see that activity. Whether Walton is correct about this or not (and I believe he isn't), a case can be made that the kind of communication involved in hardcore pornography is distinctively different from paradigm cases of speech that a free speech principle is intended to protect.

There are independent arguments about why adults who want it should have free access to this sort of imagery, and perhaps governments should not legislate against such material provided no one is harmed in its production. Certainly this is true of non-violent pornography. Millions of people get a great deal of pleasure from this and for some people this is their principal source of sexual satisfaction. On this view, however, these are not *free speech* arguments. If pornography isn't in any sense speech or communication, the argument goes, it should be treated as a separate moral issue. This is a position taken by Frederick Schauer. He used a slightly different argument to reach this conclusion. His point is that a hardcore film may be the equivalent of a vibrator: 'At its most extreme, hard core pornography is a sex aid, no more and no less ...'. For him use of hardcore pornography is tantamount to actual sexual activity. Although arousal is achieved by means of visual material rather than by touch, this is irrelevant: neither sex aids nor hardcore pornography communicate in the way that language or pictures typically do. Hardcore pornography is a sexual surrogate and a form of sexual stimulation. If Schauer is right about this, then hardcore pornography has little to do with free speech.

Catherine MacKinnon, who has campaigned for many years against pornography, also rejects the idea that pornography should be protected by a principle of free speech. With Andrea Dworkin she was responsible for an Ordinance that was briefly adopted in Indianapolis that would have made it illegal to make, publish, and sell pornography—the Ordinance was later ruled unconstitutional on First Amendment grounds. She suggests in her book *Only Words* that hardcore pornography is an act of subordination of women, not just an expression, and so should be excluded from discussions about free speech altogether. For her it is a 'lie' that pornography is speech. If a precise enough definition of pornography is given, she maintains, it can be clearly distinguished from the kinds of communication which do merit free speech protection in the areas of political, education, artistic, and literary expression. In her opinion even engaging in discussion about whether or not pornography should be considered a free speech issue can be damaging:

8. Catherine MacKinnon

> To take the claim seriously enough even to rebut it that this practice of sexual violation and inequality, this medium of slave traffic, is an opinion or a discussion is to collaborate, to some degree, in the legal and intellectual fraudulence of its position. It is to treat this position as what it pretends to be, one side in a bona fide discussion, rather than as what it is, a legitimizing smokescreen for sexual exploitation.

In contrast to these views, however, pornographic images and pornographic films *can* be used to communicate ideas, either directly or indirectly, even though they often don't. The ideas expressed by pornography may not always be profound, and some of the ideas may be offensive to many. These may be ideas about sexual liberation, or they may be subversive ideas about the roles of men or women; or they may even be provocative about the limits of censorship. But pornography, including hardcore pornography, can on occasion express thoughts that should be permitted to enter the market place of ideas. Furthermore it is a tenet of liberalism that if you are committed to free speech and toleration of diversity then you should not censor any view merely because you find it offensive, distasteful, or trivial or because you disagree with it, or because it is morally repugnant to you. That would be to prejudge it before it has had a chance to contribute to the debate. The state should be neutral between competing ideas, otherwise a form of censorship limits what enters the market place of ideas to the detriment of everyone. All that should concern government is whether the expression causes or instigates actual harm against other people.

A feminist defence of pornography

The pro-pornography feminist Wendy McElroy, however, has gone further than argue for the toleration of pornography. On the basis of her own experience and extensive research into the pornography industry, she maintains that pornography's existence is on balance beneficial to women. In her book *XXX: A Woman's Right to Pornography* (1995) she argues for an individualist feminism that puts great weight on personal choice. She believes that women (and men) should not be denied access to pornography and should be free to make up their own minds about whether this is something they wish to use. In her view, pornography can benefit women in at least three ways: (1) pornography gives a panoramic view of sexual possibilities; (2) pornography allows viewers to experience and imaginatively explore sexual alternatives safely; and (3) pornography provides different sorts of information about sexual interaction from textbooks; pornography allows the viewer to explore their emotional response to a fantasized scenario. If she is right about this, then hardcore pornography is not simply a kind of sex aid, but can be of cognitive importance, since it allows viewers to learn about themselves, and so is not absolutely beyond the scope of any general free speech principle. Overall, she suggests, suppression of hardcore pornography would restrict women's choices rather than, as writers such as MacKinnon claim, enlarge them.

This view contrasts directly with the views of those feminists such as MacKinnon who believe that pornography should be much more tightly censored than it is, or else banned altogether. This is principally because of the physical, psychological, and societal harms that may arise from its availability.

Physical and psychological harm to participants

There are a number of ways in which people may be harmed by pornography. First there is harm to actors in making pornography. The most straightforward case is where actors are injured, raped, or otherwise coerced to perform acts against their will, some of which may lead to the physical harm of sexually transmitted disease as well as to severe psychological harms. Like other sex trade workers, pornographic actors are particularly vulnerable to physical abuse and may find it difficult to be taken seriously by the police because of the nature of their work. Linda Lovelace described in her autobiography *Ordeal* how she had been beaten by her husband and forced at gunpoint to perform during the making of the film *Deep Throat*, perhaps the best-known pornographic film of all time and one that achieved crossover distribution in major cinemas. These are clear cases of harm, and would be covered by laws against coercion and rape. A principle of freedom of speech cannot be used to defend actual harm and coercion. The situation is further complicated because performing in pornography may be a last resort for people *in extremis*, and some participants may be particularly vulnerable and find it very difficult to say no to any request no matter how degrading or painful. Catherine MacKinnon has claimed that pornography is made 'overwhelmingly by poor, desperate, homeless, pimped women who were sexually abused as children'.

The argument that hardcore pornography often involves direct physical harm and coercion and so should be outlawed is in part an empirical one. It turns on alleged facts about the pornography industry that may be difficult to uncover and probably only apply to some sections of it. The claims about psychological harms are hard to assess. The classic liberal position of Mill doesn't recognize psychological harms as genuine harms. Yet 150 years later we are far more sensitive to the serious damage to an individual that psychological abuse can inflict. It would be absurd never to consider psychological harms as a reason for curtailing free speech. Yet, once again we meet with the difficulty of assessing where to draw the line: when is psychological harm of sufficient severity to merit it trumping rights to free speech? Acknowledging that such line drawing may be difficult is not to say that it is impossible. Clear guidelines could in principle be given and applied here.

Usually the question of harm caused to participants—whether physical or psychological or both—is only one of a group of connected arguments that are used in favour of outlawing some pornography. One of the most important of these is that watching pornography may cause people to commit sex crimes they would not otherwise have committed.

Pornography and rape

Some rapists and sexual sadists are heavy users of hardcore pornography and in particular cases this undoubtedly fuels their fantasies and shapes their behaviour. It is, however, extremely difficult to produce conclusive evidence about causal connections between using pornography and the likelihood of committing a sex crime. If a straightforward causal link between watching pornography and causing others harm could be proved, then this would be a *prima facie* ground for censorship; however, the results of scientific research in this area are not conclusive. The difficulty lies in establishing that the pornography was to a large degree the cause of the crime or a major contributory factor and that this is not just a correlation.

Correlation and cause should not be confused. Pornography is very widely used by the general population, most of whom never commit a sex crime.

Catherine MacKinnon suggests a hypothetical mechanism by which pornography encourages rape: users of violent pornography become sexually habituated by means of a rewarding kind of conditioning. They get the visual stimulation from watching a film of a particular violent sexual act, they get the reward from the sexual arousal that accompanies it. It is as if watching a video of a violent sexual act is a training for performing that act on a victim in reality. MacKinnon maintains that

> Sooner or later, in one way or another, the consumers want to live out the pornography further in three dimensions. Sooner or later, in one way or another they do. *It* makes them want to; when they believe they can, when they feel they can get away with it, *they* do.

This is a rhetorical exaggeration, but the mechanism she describes may turn out to be a significant factor for some criminals. As a generalization, though, it is clearly false. Many regular users of pornography will never move beyond pornography, nor will they behave immorally in their real sexual encounters. A very high percentage of the population use pornography at some point in their lives. It is scarcely credible that these people will all be conditioned to behave in the extreme way that MacKinnon describes.

The point that questions of censorship turn on empirical research about pornography's actual link with harm was made very clearly in the *Williams Report on Obscenity and Film Censorship* (1979), which made public the findings of a group chaired by the philosopher Bernard Williams:

The presumption in favour of freedom of expression is strong, but it is a presumption, and it can be overruled by considerations of harms which the speech or publication in question may cause.

While the jury is out on the empirical evidence, this argument for censoring pornography is not conclusive. However, because there is a strong likelihood of there being some connection between violent pornography and real violence, it seems prudent to suggest some restrictions on violence in pornography.

Societal harms

Feminist arguments against pornography tend to focus on heterosexual pornography directed at a male consumer—typically this would take the form of photographs in magazines and films which may be delivered in the form of videos, DVDs, downloaded or streamed via the Internet, or in movie theatres. Homosexual and bisexual pornography, whether produced by and for men or women, is rarely mentioned.

Heterosexual pornography often communicates offensive messages about the sexual availability of women and allegedly legitimizes their objectification; this is one reason why so many feminists oppose it. It may also present women with particular body types, surgically enhanced breasts, for instance, creating false expectations about real women in male consumers. Some pornography is also degrading to all women by its nature, as for example, pornography in which women are portrayed as humiliated or subjected to sexual violence, particularly when they are represented as enjoying it. There is presumed to be a generalizing effect here with one woman's enjoyment of sexual humiliation on film being read as emblematic of all women's attitudes. The woman in the film, by a kind of synecdoche, stands in for all women. The presumed result is that a misleading picture of what women want is given support: at its extreme there is a message that all women get sexual enjoyment from being used roughly and hurt, that all women enjoy being raped, or treated as sex slaves: a view that seems likely to have dangerous consequences for real women.

Liberals, such as Ronald Dworkin, however, argue that most pornography should not be censored, unless people are directly harmed in its making, such as when children are involved, or where there is coercion of adults rather than free choice: 'The essence of negative liberty is freedom to offend, and that applies to the tawdry as well as the heroic'.

The typical liberal position is this: paternalism, protecting people for their own good, is entirely appropriate towards children and young people, and this might involve insisting that pornography is never displayed in places where children might or could encounter it. But adults who choose to use or make pornography should be free to do so up to the point where someone else is harmed. Different people make good and bad choices about their own lives, but it is not, many liberals believe, for the state to decide for them whether or not they seek sexual titillation or satisfaction through using pornography. The state should be as neutral as possible between different ways of living, provided that they don't result in direct harm to other people:

> Liberals defend pornography, though most of them despise it, in
> order to defend a conception of the First Amendment that includes,
> as at least one of its purposes, protecting equality in the processes
> through which the moral as well as the political environment is
> formed.

Furthermore, in the area of free speech, there is a fear that making any special case for censorship is dangerous: it can be the first step down a slippery slope that legitimizes far broader censorship than was originally intended or justified. Every curtailment of free speech, even of speech that is repulsive to many, carries the risk that democracy and individual self-expression may both soon be at stake.

Even if pornography does bring about greater costs than benefits to society and particularly to women, it doesn't necessarily follow that it should be censored. It is extremely difficult for a censor to suppress just the material that is corrupting. There is a real danger that the censor will cut too deep and excise material that is culturally valuable in the act of preventing access to the most trivial and empty kinds of pornography. That would be a high cost. A safer course might be to risk tolerating some pernicious pornography rather than inadvertently destroy works which subsequent generations would have found important.

The legal moralist's approach to pornography

The liberal approach attacked by MacKinnon stands in contrast to that of legal moralists, such as Lord Devlin: those who believe that the law should enshrine societal values to the extent that anything which is morally corrupting or might be seen to undermine the traditional family and family values should be forbidden by law. This may be motivated by religious beliefs about how all human beings should live, or by conservative secular ones.

Pornography's existence and availability outrages and disgusts many. It is morally indecent, they tell us, and the world would be a much better place if its production and consumption were outlawed. The moral fabric of society is damaged by pornography's availability. Therefore, on this view, the state is justified in intervening. Indeed, it has a duty to do so. Moral legalists believe that the role of the state is in part to ensure the survival of a culture, a moral climate, a way of life. Individual freedom is not a value that should be allowed priority over traditional family values, such as those that most Christians subscribe to and most Christian apologists preach (even if they don't always practise them). For such opponents of pornography, no defence based on a free speech principle would be acceptable. Other values have a far higher status.

The approach of censoring pornography for the sake of the potential consumer and for society at large is a form of paternalism directed towards adults. Those who advocate it would be happy to see the law shape behaviour. They believe that moral harms are genuine harms and want to prevent them occurring; critics argue that it would be improper for governments to make judgements between competing views of the good life. Governments, on that view, should tolerate pluralism, not impose one form of morality on their citizens.

Those advocating traditional family values and opposing pornography on the basis of them, have allies amongst some contemporary feminists. Not because the two groups share a range of fundamental values about the nature of the family—far from it—but rather because many feminists would, like the moralists, be happy to see pornography eradicated, in their case because of the harm—direct, indirect, physical, and psychological—that it can, they believe, cause women.

This is an empirical hypothesis that involves a prediction about what would happen if access to pornography were more tightly controlled or prevented altogether, namely that greater equality between the sexes would be achieved. Set in the historical context of systematic sexism and the largely hidden history of men's sexual abuse of women, this might be one way of redressing the balance, though the argument rests on the accuracy of the hypothesis about the effects of banning pornography. Here there is thought to be a tension between free speech that tolerates the production and use of pornography and a commitment to sexual equality that seems to require that hardcore pornography be made illegal.

The goals of freedom and equality cannot always both be achieved. The difficult question is how much weight to give to the different values.

This is a recurrent issue when discussing free speech. The freedom of speakers and audiences to hear what they wish to hear needs to be balanced against the interests of those who don't want to hear what is being said, who are offended, disgusted, outraged, or feel violated and degraded by the message.

Those who defend a free speech principle usually believe that there should be a presumption of free speech and that any restriction on it needs to be based on more than a gut reaction of disgust. It needs to be argued, backed by evidence, and clearly not a step down a slippery slope that makes more serious censorship likely or even inevitable. Yet almost every defender of free speech wishes to draw the line somewhere. This line drawing, when subjected to close scrutiny, is rarely completely consistent since it involves resisting very strong pre-existing intuitions for most of us.

Most liberals are vulnerable to a charge of inconsistency here when it comes to the censorship of pornography depicting children engaged in sexual activity. When, as is typical, children are abused or raped in the production of child pornography, there are obvious harm-based liberal arguments about why this should be banned. But when computer-generated images of children are the basis of child pornography the situation is more complicated. This is essentially a form of collage, and the obscene collage can be generated from innocuous family snaps. Few people would want to tolerate such imagery, but for a consequentialist the reasoning has to be based on empirical evidence about the likely harm caused by allowing such imagery to be made and freely circulated. It seems obvious that there are strong links between making and consuming such imagery and an actual risk of harm to children; but many people feel there are equally strong links between the making and consumption of certain sorts of adult pornography and actual risk of harm to women. The strongest liberal position here would be to maintain that, repugnant as such computer-generated images are, they should be tolerated unless empirical evidence of their link to actual harm to children can be demonstrated. Yet here it seems highly unlikely that the benefits of free speech would outweigh its costs. Most of us would feel happier if such imagery were outlawed because of the likely connection it has with paedophilic fantasy, and ultimately with fuelling the desire of those who may well go on to harm children.

Art and pornography

Are there any good reasons why Robert Mapplethorpe's sexually explicit photography, the Chapman Brothers' sculptures, or Vladimir Nabokov's *Lolita* should be immune from censorship to which they might fall prey if they weren't created by artists or acknowledged writers? Is there a special case that can be made about the arts that exempts them from censorship? One response is that artists should be immune from censorship because of the seriousness of their attempts to engage with the human condition and because of the literary or artistic qualities of interpretation of events that complicate the experience of such works. In our culture we rightly privilege the role of artist because it is through art that culture is transmitted and interrogated.

Perhaps the most important case in which an artistic defence was used was the *Lady Chatterley* trial in the United Kingdom. This trial, which took place in 1960, was to determine whether or not D. H. Lawrence's novel could be published in Britain or should remain banned under the Obscene Publications Act. More than fifty expert witnesses were called to testify to the literary merits of the book, including E. M. Forster, Raymond Williams, and Richard Hoggart. By general consensus, *Lady Chatterley's Lover* is far from Lawrence's best book, but the witnesses made a good case for its literary merits, conscious that they were defending a writer's freedom to express his view of life as much as defending a particular book. The book, with its repeated use of the word 'fuck' and detailed description of adultery, was certainly potentially offensive to many readers. The test for obscenity, though, was that it would corrupt and deprave readers. The judge in the case ruled that the book could be published (but not before asking the jury whether they thought they'd be happy for their servants to read it).

In 1990 the photographer Robert Mapplethorpe's exhibition *The Perfect Moment* was shown at the Contemporary Arts Center in Cincinnati. The exhibition included explicit images of homosexual sado-masochism, male on male oral sex, and also a photograph, *Rosie* (1976), which was of a 4-year-old girl sitting on a garden bench wearing a skirt that clearly revealed her exposed genitals. The director of the museum Dennis Barrie was charged with obscenity and the misuse of a minor in pornography. The image was not included when the show moved to London's Hayward Gallery. As with the *Lady Chatterley* trial, questions of artistic merit were central. Dennis Barrie was acquitted on the grounds that Mapplethorpe's work demonstrated erotic artistry.

Mapplethorpe's photography is often beautiful and highly formal even when his subjects are engaged in explicit hardcore sado-masochistic activities. His case might also have been made easier by widespread knowledge of his own homosexuality. In an interview he explained how he wanted to use obscenity, but at the same time transcend it:

> it could be pornography and still have redeeming social value. It can be both, which is my whole point in doing it—to have all the elements of pornography and yet have a structure of lighting that makes it go beyond what it is.

The question raised by both the *Lady Chatterley* trial and the Mapplethorpe trial, though, is whether a judgement of artistic merit should be a factor in determining whether or not a book, image, film, or performance should be censored.

The most libertarian approach is to argue that all artistic censorship is wrong. On this view artists should be free to challenge whatever they wish to challenge, and to express themselves however they see fit, with or without artistry. Such a position is easier to assert as a slogan than to justify. This is particularly so in the area of sexualized images of children. Where children are harmed in the production of such images, there is no need to relate this to questions of free speech. But even where children are not physically harmed, as in the Mapplethorpe case, many (and I am among them) will feel the risk of stimulating the perverse imaginations of paedophiles is too high a price to pay for artistic freedom. For others, though, repugnant as such an image may seem to them, it should be tolerated. It is easy to tolerate the art you like—the real test of whether you are sincere about free speech is when you are prepared to tolerate the art you find repugnant and deeply offensive. Toleration, of course, does not preclude opposition short of censorship.

In her account of this case in her book *Eroticism and Art*, the art historian Alyce Mahon seems surprised that the photograph caused consternation

> ... despite the fact that the model, Rosie, a grown woman aged 23 at the time of the show, had no problem with her portrait and happily displayed it in Notting Hill, London, at the restaurant she managed.

The actual retrospective consent of the model is not, however, the issue here. Imagine the case where Rosie had in fact as an adult felt deeply ashamed of this widely reproduced image. She was not of an age where she could possibly have given informed consent to be photographed at the time the image was made. Although she was not physically harmed in the process, had she been severely traumatized by the public display of the image, this could have amounted to a psychological harm. Mapplethorpe could not have known that she would later be proud of the photograph rather than disturbed by it. The lack of possibility of consent in such a case makes this very different from an image of an adult taken with that adult's consent.

A beautifully shot and skilfully printed photograph of a 4-year-old girl's genitals is still a photograph that could easily arouse a paedophile and its public display might also indirectly communicate the idea that a sexual gaze up a 4-year-old's skirt is socially acceptable. For this reason I would not condone its exhibition. Given the context of an exhibition containing photographs of overtly sexual acts, it would be disingenuous to claim that there is no suggestion of sexuality in the image *Rosie*. The juxtaposition with photographs of people having various kinds of sex makes a sexual reading almost inevitable. It is reasonable to question the motives of an artist who creates and exhibits such an image; it is also right to be concerned about the probable effects of displaying such an image. The risks associated with this photograph and others like it, is, for me, far too high to give it the benefit of the doubt. Indeed, there is something disturbing about the view that the artistic expression and merit of this image should make it immune from other considerations, as if artistic concerns always trump moral ones.

Most liberal defenders of free speech argue for a formal principle that concentrates on the protection of speech that is neutral about the ideas being expressed (up to the point where they instigate harm). In the cases just described, though, the artistic merit of the works in question was taken to be relevant. Had the courts demonstrated that either Lawrence's book or Mapplethorpe's images were totally lacking in artistic merit, then they would very likely have been banned. But why should artistic merit be relevant?

One answer is that artistic works express and embody thoughts about whatever they describe or depict. On this view the aim of a pornographic work is to be transparent to what is in front of the lens. Pornography is a kind of voyeurism. In contrast art that superficially resembles pornography always interposes interpretation and imaginative engagement with the subject matter. It may, as Susan Sontag has argued, portray what she called 'the pornographic imagination', as for example in a novel that portrayed a paedophile or a sexual sadist.

Lady Chatterley's Lover is not written in such a way simply to arouse the reader; Mapplethorpe's images aren't made simply as pornography, but are intended to be seen as beautiful formally, and as having some of the same qualities as classical art. On this sort of argument it is the possibility of reflective understanding or of presentation of a character that these works provide the viewer or reader that takes them beyond pornography and allows them to be treated differently. A photograph of a 4-year-old girl taken by a paedophile would clearly constitute a kind of abuse. On this argument, Mapplethorpe should be treated differently from the paedophile because his artistry allowed him to produce an image that is about innocence and beauty rather than a focus of sexual stimulation. A pragmatic difficulty with this sort of approach, though, is distinguishing the artist from a paedophile wishing to work under the protection of a principle that protects erotic art.

Another argument for treating art as a protected zone is that art by its very nature is an area of human endeavour that presents serious and important challenges to received opinion. Restrictions on artistic freedom are on this view particularly pernicious

9. *Piss Christ*, by Andres Serrano

because they curb the creativity of the very people who keep our culture alive, self-reflective, and self-critical.

Yet this approach is antithetical to any free market of ideas approach to free speech: it assumes that one area of expression should be protected above others. This sort of immunity from censorship has also been invoked in the area of art that offends people's religious sensibilities. Two cases suffice to make this point; both were considered offensive. When Andres Serrano submerged a crucifix in his own urine and photographed this as *Piss Christ* many Christians were deeply offended by this deliberately provocative work. Indeed, questions were asked in the US Senate about the appropriateness of this artist winning public funding for his work. Some of those who derided *Piss Christ* claimed that Serrano wasn't an artist, perhaps indirectly acknowledging an argument that art merits special protection from censorship.

Similarly, although at first glance Chris Ofili's 1996 image of Mary is inoffensive enough the Virgin's right breast is constructed from elephant dung, and the background is decorated with photographs of body parts cut from pornographic magazines. Again, many Christians found this work offensive. When it travelled to the Brooklyn Museum of Art as part of the *Sensation* exhibition in 1999, the then mayor of New York, Rudolph Giuliani, was one who was outraged at this potent combination of apparent blasphemy and sexually explicit imagery. He took it to be an attack specifically on Roman Catholicism and threatened to withhold seven million dollars of public funding from the museum because of it, though he was later forced to back down.

Many in the artworld were appalled by the attempt to censor art. Art should be immune from this sort of criticism, they claimed.

But there is a good argument that the act of censorship is what was wrong, not the fact that it was art that was censored. In a civilized society freedom to offend should be protected, but there are not good grounds for making art a special case and protecting it from censorship simply because it is art.

Chapter 5
Free speech in the age of the Internet

Has the Internet changed everything?

John Stuart Mill was writing in the 1850s, yet his writing on free speech is still the starting point for most discussions of the topic today. Immense technological changes in communication have occurred since then. The Internet has transformed our world. It has democratized comment, massively expanded the reach of any message, and opened people up to new ideas and new ways of interacting with each other, whether by email, weblog, podcast, vodcast, chat room, or in the persona of an avatar in *Second Life*.

Where once publishers and newspaper editors policed the gates of access to a wider public, today the rise of citizen journalism has demonstrated that almost anyone with an Internet connection and very basic knowledge of computing can reach a very large audience without any intermediaries controlling what they say. The future of free speech must be tied to the ways in which individuals are permitted by governments to use the Internet (and to the practical limits governments have in exercising control over how their citizens do this). Whether governments or others are practically capable of restricting free expression in the age of the Internet is an important question. But even if they can't make a significant difference in this respect, the moral question remains of whether or not such a proliferation of expressed ideas is good for humanity. Are there particular dangers associated with the Internet?

Some dangers of the Internet

Richard Posner has identified four features of this new means of dissemination that may be thought to magnify the dangers of irresponsible speech and so should have an influence on how we think about free expression.

Anonymity. The Internet permits users and creators of communications to remain hidden. This makes it far easier to produce, create and consume false, illegal, and dangerous material such as child pornography or hate speech.

Lack of quality control. Almost anyone can post almost anything on the Internet. This is very different from conventional publishing where much inaccurate and misleading information is filtered out by the publishing system or removed at the request of lawyers before a book, magazine, or newspaper goes to press. On the Internet unsubstantiated assertions are as easily published as well-researched articles. Indeed, a whole genre of so-called Gripe Sites has grown up with the sole purpose of expressing grudges, often in libellous form. Rumours about celebrities, frequently unsubstantiated or completely false, are spread virally via weblogs; had such views been expressed in published newspapers, then many of them would have been quashed by legal pressure.

Huge potential audience. The Internet provides access to millions of potential readers and viewers across the world. This can magnify any harm caused by speech.

Antisocial people find their soul mates. People with odd, eccentric, subversive, and dangerous views can find each other very easily on the Internet. Where in the past someone with such views would have been socially isolated, today, linked by chat rooms and websites, such people 'become emboldened not only to express their ideas, but also to act upon them, their self-confidence bolstered by membership in a community of believers'.

Anonymity, as Posner notes, need not be a permanent aspect of the medium. It may be a transitory feature. Nevertheless, it is a present-day feature. This has a practical implication: it is extremely difficult to restrict some kinds of expression on the Internet and even harder to track down the creators and users of material. For those willing to use unscrupulous methods, the Internet has greatly increased freedom to communicate across the world because the risks of being traced are lower than with conventional modes of publishing ideas. Even if we believe that some views are so hateful or likely to incite violence that they should, ideally, be censored, there are severe practical difficulties in carrying out this censorship. From a moral point of view we will want to condemn incitements to violence, but pragmatically we may not be able to prevent their expression on the Internet. If censorship is practically impossible, we will need to develop other methods of minimizing the damage caused by this kind of expression.

On the second point, the lack of quality control, this is rapidly changing. Many websites control quality. That is the basis of their reputation and readership. Also, the quality control often comes after publication in the form of certification by sites with a high reputation usually due to affiliation to a university, a trusted organization such as the BBC or *The New York Times*, or a public body. Some websites, such as *Arts and Letters Daily* (www.aldaily.com) aggregate links to high-quality material and so sift what is available to the reader, thus producing the equivalent of a literary magazine. Again, as Posner notes, lack of quality control, to the extent that it now exists, is probably a transitory aspect of the Internet. The consequence, though, is that there are already many potentially damaging assertions being circulated widely that would not have been circulated by conventional published media. For those who have faith in the free market of ideas, the diversity and range of expression is a good consequence of the medium; for others, though, this is a worrying product of new technology. The same medium that can allow the swift dissemination of information about humanitarian issues can be used to promote suicide bombing, or to spread false and damaging rumours about film stars' private lives with little chance of redress.

The huge potential audience for ideas and images certainly magnifies the possible effects of publication. I can post a message at almost no cost on my weblog from my home and it can be found, read, and responded to within seconds by people on the other side of the world. This is certainly a worrying aspect of the Internet as well as one of its chief benefits. The cost of such immediacy and range may be great as Posner points out: 'A nut who couldn't get a newspaper to publish any of his letters to it can reach thousands or even millions of people over the Internet at virtually zero cost'.

What this means is that any damaging speech can be much more dangerous than at any point in history. This is undeniable. Yet, the possibility of publishing responses swiftly and with just as large a readership to some degree counters this. Speech can be met with counter-speech and far fewer possible contributors to any debate are excluded. Also, a wider range of views can be expressed than would be possible in mainstream conventional media.

Posner's fourth point, that dangerous antisocial people can link up with those who share their views and bolster each other's ideas, is surely correct. This again has great potential to bring about real harm. Paedophiles have teamed up in this way, as have terrorists.

Usually the activity of such people is clearly illegal. But the ease of communication and the networks that allow similar people to find each other have facilitated connections that have led directly to violence. Less dramatically, but still with very serious, often fatal, consequences, teenage anorexics have been very active in exchanging ideas for weight loss and for overcoming the pangs of hunger and have reinforced dangerous ideals of thinness and of the evils of eating. The risk in this last sort of case is to the vulnerable people drawn to the pro-anorexic websites. It is true that the same technology that permits antisocial people to combine forces also permits those whose aims are good to discuss and collaborate to oppose evil. Nevertheless, whoever champions completely unfettered communication needs to be clear about how serious the consequences of that approach may now be. In view of these sort of risks, some have argued that Internet Service Providers (ISPs) should be held legally responsible for the content they make accessible. Yet if this approach were taken many of the benefits of immediacy and openness of communication would be lost. Ultimately the right decision in this situation must be based on a very complex and ever-changing cost-benefit analysis that takes into account how the Internet is actually being used, what is possible given the developing technology, and what the actual consequences of different courses of action are likely to be.

The 'Daily Me'?

Cass Sunstein has raised a different concern about the impact of the Internet and associated technologies on free speech. The benefits to democracy of free speech in part derive from the public having access to a wide range of speakers and opinions. The underlying assumption is that through encountering views with which they disagree, members of the public will focus their own beliefs, and develop their critical engagement with the issues that concern them. Without exposure to a range of positions, individuals may become complacent in their views; they may not even realize that their views are controversial or widely despised.

Sunstein makes the point that for a heterogeneous society to function well people should be exposed to materials that they would not have chosen to read or listen to:

> Unanticipated encounters, involving topics and points of view that people have not sought out and perhaps find quite irritating, are central to democracy and even to freedom itself.

This is connected with the idea that for a deliberative democracy to function citizens must be capable of reflection and debate about the issues that concern them as well as be able to call their elected representatives to account. Also if the tradition of meeting speech with counter-speech is to function, then the counter-speech must be heard, particularly by the people speakers are responding to.

The Internet facilitates a highly selective approach to the information that we receive. We can filter out whatever we don't wish to know about. Furthermore we can do this automatically with software that recognizes our interests, likes, and dislikes. In principle each person could tailor news, entertainment, and every other kind of material they receive from the Internet to their particular tastes, not just in terms of subject matter, but also in the stance taken by the writer or presenter. A liberal could only hear news with a liberal spin, a racist need never have his or her views challenged by anything that comes via the Internet. The Internet user would every day receive the 'Daily Me'—a personally adapted selection. If large numbers of people were to have such personally selected access to other people's ideas, Sunstein suggests, the conditions for a healthy democracy would not be met. This is not an argument for forcing individuals to use the Internet in a prescribed way—that would be an unacceptable instance of paternalism. But the Internet exacerbates the risks of only hearing what you want to hear.

In response to Sunstein, it could be argued that we all filter our exposure to ideas now. I don't subscribe to racist magazines, nor do I read books about homoeopathy. I read newspapers that I find sympathetic in their editorial stance, and mix with people who broadly share many of my views. In my reading on the Internet, partly because much of the content is free, partly because it is so easy to access, and partly because of the neutrality of search engines when listing items on a topic, I have in fact read a wider range of opinions than I probably would if it didn't exist. And because the Internet encourages dialogue rather than simply passive reception of ideas, through comment functions on weblogs and discussion in chat rooms and so on, whenever I have posted anything controversial on a weblog I have had comments which fall into the category of counter-speech: responses from those who hold a very different set of beliefs. This is an anecdotal response, but it suggests that Sunstein's concerns about how the Internet might narrow minds need empirical investigation to establish whether this is in fact how people tend to use the Internet.

Paternalism towards children

A further worrying aspect of the Internet is that it makes it very difficult to control children's access to, for example, pornographic material, and to ways of interacting with strangers, with all the attendant risks. This may again be a transitory aspect of the medium. Perhaps more sophisticated child controls will reduce these risks in the near future. But at present there could be grounds for outlawing some kinds of website as a matter of child protection even if this limits free speech for some adults. For example, as already mentioned, there are many pro-anorexia and pro-self-harm websites and chat rooms that allow young people to exchange ideas about how to lose weight and reaffirm these people's false views about their bodies in ways which could ultimately contribute to their deaths. Many pornographic websites are easy for children to access. While there may be arguments for tolerating this sort of website if its use were restricted to adults, paternalism towards children is entirely appropriate. If there were a simple way to bar children and adolescents from having access to such sites, this would be a good solution. But in the absence of such a reliable means of exclusion, the least worst option would presumably be to outlaw such sites and to take strong action to make sure that they are not available on the grounds that they carry with them a very significant risk to children.

Using other people's words and images

The existence of the Internet has also brought to the fore concerns about the limits on free speech that copyright law imposes. There have been prohibitions on using other people's words without permission (or in many cases payment) for hundreds of years. Copyright is a compromise between the needs of writers to receive financial reward for their writing and the needs of users of their works. The result of copyright law, which differs from country to country, is that there are many words that it would be illegal to publish, speak, or perform. This is potentially a restriction on freedom of speech, particularly if you are a writer who wishes to collage other people's writing, or you desire to perform a speech from a contemporary playwright's work in a public place without permission.

In recent years, the ease with which digital technology permits reuse and re-versioning of other people's writing has raised new issues about freedom and led to campaigns for reform in copyright laws to allow freer use of other people's words.

T. S. Eliot's poem 'The Wasteland' famously combines original lines with 'stolen' ones. A new context gives them new meanings and links place and poem to the past, often with irony. For Eliot it was obvious that great literature builds on and uses the literature of the past. The meaning of any piece of writing in part derives from its relation to other writing, and particularly to the writing of those now dead, who constitute a particular tradition. In his poetic practice he went further and actually embedded fragments of this tradition within his own poetry, adding footnotes to show sources.

William Shakespeare used plots from historical sources or built on the ideas of his contemporaries. Musicians frequently quote from other composers. Visual collage is often a reuse of other people's creative work, but the result is typically a new work. In almost every art form the great creators build on and reuse the work of their predecessors—sometimes in a disguised way, but often blatantly. Indeed, selective quotation is a major trope of postmodernism. That, many people believe, is how art evolves. Creativity comes from a relationship with the art of the past. Furthermore, art is an area that demands freedom—it is where individuals push at boundaries of conformity. Every restriction cuts off a possible branch of artistic development. Much of this reusing of the past is appropriate; but some is morally culpable in that the creators deliberately give the impression that they have produced the words and not their predecessors.

Postmodern art practice is at least as magpie-like and eclectic as T. S. Eliot was in 'The Wasteland'. In one extreme case the artist Sherrie Levine re-photographed well-known photographs by Walker Evans from an exhibition catalogue of his work. Levine exhibited her prints, which were basically photographic reproductions of Evans's. It could be argued that her use of these images was very different from Evans's, contributing a range of ideas to the work. Indeed, most commentators have argued that this kind of open appropriation should be seen as a postmodern comment on notions of originality, authorship, and authenticity in photography. To this extent she is principally a conceptual artist. But, visibly, her work, which, ironically, is now collected by major art galleries, is heavily parasitic on the original images taken by Walker Evans. Indeed its parasitical nature is essential to what it is.

Free speech vs copyright

But there may be legal (as well as moral) restrictions on reusing other people's words and images. Not all words. Many of the words Eliot appropriated in 'The Wasteland', such as those by Shakespeare, were long out of copyright. We don't know all that much about Shakespeare the man, but we do know that he died more than seventy years ago, so his works are all now in the public domain, i.e. freely available for use by all. By re-contextualizing them, Eliot gave them new meaning, but readers were meant to appreciate the source. There is no attempt to pass these words off as his own—that would be plagiarism even though the words are out of copyright.

But where works are in copyright there are extensive legal restrictions on freedom of speech. Copyright protects the expression of ideas, the particular words (or images) used. But it does not protect ideas themselves. This is an important distinction. What this means is that you are not free to speak or write someone else's words, though you are in many circumstances free to paraphrase them. The ideas can be expressed in other words, but you may not quote at length in public without the rightsholder's permission.

In the UK as soon as a work is written down it is automatically protected by copyright. So if I write a novel in my bedsit, put it in a drawer, and forget about it, if you find it and publish it without my permission, you infringe my copyright. Even though I hadn't registered it or shown it to anyone else it would still have legal protection as my intellectual property.

But my rights in my novel don't just extend to control over whether I allow you to publish it. If you gave a reading without my permission, you would also be infringing my copyright. Similarly if you adapted the work in some way. Or even if you chose to lend the copy out for a fee.

I also have what are misleadingly termed 'moral rights' in relation to my work. Although called 'moral' these are legal rights that I have as creator of the work. These are:

> *The right of attribution*, which includes the right to be identified as author of the work.
> *The right of integrity*. This is the right not to have my work adapted or treated in a defamatory or derogatory way.

If I want to express myself using other people's words (or images), perhaps by collaging them, or performing them, or cutting and pasting them on to a website, then I can't; or at least not without risk of being sued for infringing copyright. This is one of the less frequently discussed aspects of free speech, but it is becoming increasingly important in the age of the Internet and digital media. Cut and paste options are standard word-processing packages and very young children operate them efficiently. Handheld digital photocopiers, digital cameras, scanners, and so on make reusing other creators' work quite literally child's play. But the law in most countries of the world prevents some reuse of other people's intellectual and artistic labours, no matter how creative the outcome.

There are exemptions here. For example, the notion of Fair Dealing allows in the UK selective quotation for the purposes of criticism or review. In the USA there is a more extensive notion of Fair Use. But these exceptions typically will not permit substantial use of another's work, even with acknowledgement, and in the areas of poetry and song lyrics, quoting a single line could constitute an infringement. Since 2003 fair dealing in the UK for the purposes of research and private study does not extend to any commercial activity: in other words, you cannot claim an exception to copyright law under fair dealing if you gain commercially from using the work in this way. What this means in practice, for example, is that a biographer may be thwarted in his or her attempt to make public the contents of a long-dead subject's letters. Provided that the letters are still in copyright, the writer's estate can determine whether or not these may be used in a published work. The biographer will not be free to use certain words that his or her subject actually used: copyright will prevent that. And this restriction could last for seventy years after the death of the person in question.

The movement to reform copyright law

Laurence Lessig, a law professor with a special interest in intellectual property in the age of the Internet, has made a passionate case for rethinking copyright legislation. He argues that we are in a distinctively new situation. At the very moment when copying and collaging have become easier than ever before, and everyone with access to the Internet has an enormous amount of work that they might reuse, copyright law has, perversely, extended the period of protection of rightsholders' interests. Particularly galling for Lessig and others who champion the rights of users was the so-called Sonny Bono ruling in the USA, which extended the period of time that works remain *post mortem* in copyright. Lessig is keen to produce a world in which intellectual property is available for common use.

The justification for having copyright laws at all is that they protect the interests of creators and publishers and, by making it possible to earn money from creative activity, thereby stimulate creators to create. This is a practical compromise between the interests of the two groups. Without copyright, the argument goes, writers and artists would find it extremely difficult to make a living. Many of the incentives for creativity would evaporate.

But the laws of copyright are not supposed to be biased wholly towards creators. What the legislators aim to do is balance the interests of the creators and other rightsholders (such as publishers) against the interests of users. Users need to be able to get access to the ideas and works of art of their age, and many of them will want to be able to reuse these works in part or whole. In the UK and the rest of Europe literary copyright lies with the author's estate for seventy years after the author's death before the work then enters the public domain. This is excessive by any measure and is largely the result of EU law taking the longest *post mortem* copyright law (which was Germany's) as the basis for pan-European legislation. In other words, this was another pragmatic compromise as part of a harmonization of different legal systems rather than a figure that could easily be justified on any moral grounds, or on grounds of its providing incentives for creativity.

Should those who defend free speech be joining Laurence Lessig and others in the so-called CopyLeft movement to minimize the protection of literary and other creative works and maximize their possible use? This would involve a radical overhaul of existing copyright legislation and could bite into the economic interests of writers and publishers alike.

For a consequentialist, the question underlying this debate is whether or not the increased freedom of use of other people's words brings greater benefits than the copyright status quo or some revision of it. A moderate position would be to make minor changes to existing copyright laws to produce a fairer balance that allows greater freedom of use of other people's words and images than is presently permitted, but which still provides the financial incentive to writers and artists that is so important for so many of them. This would perhaps involve a range of exceptions for creative reuse of other people's words. Such a change would be difficult to implement and police. The radical position is to lift all legal restrictions on reuse and transform the nature of intellectual property. Then the expression of an idea would immediately put it in the public domain.

From a user's position, and from that of anyone who is committed to the maximum possible freedom of speech, the radical position looks attractive. Surely it would be better for humanity if all ideas were freely in circulation made accessible by the Internet. This could unleash creativity, the argument goes. Imagine the freedom as a writer to build on the work of the great writers of the recent past, to collage it, to reprint it at will. Ideas and their expression are surely the great common heritage that we have and the more people that have access to them and freedom to use them the better.

However, there are substantial problems that would be associated with putting this into practice. Many people believe that to take the radical approach would be to risk completely undermining the economic basis of the production and distribution of written texts. The same is true for many kinds of images, such as photographs. Many writers write for some kind of recompense. Similarly, many photographers gain much of their livelihood from licensed reuses of their pictures. If there is no opportunity for them to earn money directly from reuse of their work, then a major potential source of income would evaporate. Without this sort of financial incentive, many writers too would cease to write or be forced to write much less. Economically the profession of writer is a precarious one with many writers earning substantially less than the average wage.

There is a further argument here, one based on natural justice. Why should a collager benefit so much from someone else's intellectual labour? In the area of material property those who own property are not usually obliged (except in special cases such as where a public footpath crosses their land) to allow the general public free use of what they own. Why should it be different with intellectual property, which, typically, is labour intensive to produce. Is there a good argument for treating intellectual property in a different way from material property? One major difference is that it is possible for innumerable simultaneous uses of an intellectual work, whereas not everyone could, for example, occupy a house. There are no obvious limits to the numbers of people who could simultaneously read this book, particularly if it were delivered in electronic form. One person's use does not get in the way of another's.

The issue of free speech in relation to copyright is very different from the other topics discussed in this book. In all the other cases there is a presumption of extensive free speech and any restriction on that free speech needs justification. In the case of copyright, there is a historically evolved practical solution to the problem of balancing creators' and users' interests that seems to override issues of free speech. The presumption is in favour of copyright and against free speech for those who want to use other people's words or images.

However the Internet evolves, we are living in interesting times for free speech. The compromises of the past, developed in an age of the printing press, may no longer be sustainable. New technologies are already allowing previously unimaginable opportunities for people to communicate globally. Censorship and the restriction of speech are becoming harder to implement when there are so many ways to bypass central control. In the words of Giuseppe Lampedusa: 'If we want things to stay as they are, things will have to change.'

Conclusion: the future of free speech

Plato in *The Republic* was one of the earliest philosophers to argue for severe curbs on free expression. In the ideal society that he describes, there is no room for representational art. One of his main arguments is the corrupting effect of representation or *mimesis*. For Plato reality as we perceive it is an imperfect reflection of the perfect world of The Forms, the universal types that lie behind the realm of appearance. The bed I look at is less perfect than the concept 'bed' which exists in this world of universals accessible by philosophical contemplation rather than ordinary vision. Any representation of a particular bed is necessarily imperfect since it is a depiction of something that is itself an imperfect reflection of the Form 'bed'. Plato wanted to preserve his philosopher-kings, his ideal rulers of his ideal state, from anything that might undermine their judgement of reality. Pictorial art, which was at several removes from reality, and necessarily distorted it, risked this and so was excluded.

But it wasn't just pictures that threatened the philosopher-kings' grasp of reality in Plato's utopian state: some kinds of speech, particularly the sort of poetry in which an individual took on the character of an evil person, were also corrupting, and so should similarly be banned because of their harmful effect. For Plato, then, the education of the philosopher-kings was more important than free expression. And the only way of keeping their judgement pure and accurate was to remove them from potentially damaging influences.

Although Plato's arguments against representation rely on an exotic metaphysics which is likely to find few present-day followers, Plato's heirs are ready to censor wherever they see potentially damaging words and images.

Karl Popper, writing under the shadow of Fascism in the 1940s, pointed out the totalitarian nature of Plato's thought in *The Republic*. Whether this is an accurate characterization of the whole or not, it captures the nature of Plato's curbs on free expression.

There is a degree of irony here. Plato's teacher and hero, Socrates, was tried and executed for asking questions that the Athenian state objected to. He allegedly corrupted the youth of Athens with his anti-democratic talk. He also encouraged people to worship the wrong gods. Like Jesus after him, his words were perceived as a threat, and he was duly silenced by death—in his case by drinking hemlock. But even if he had been given a reprieve on condition that he remained silent and minded his own business, Socrates valued his freedom to debate ideas above his own life.

Socrates was willing to die rather than choose a life of quietly minding his own business. In Plato's dialogue, *The Apology*, he addresses those who are about to condemn him to death:

> 'But surely, Socrates, after you have left us you can spend the rest of your life in quietly minding your own business.' This is the hardest thing of all to make some of you understand. If I say that this would be disobedience to God, and that is why I cannot 'mind my own business', you will not believe me—you'll think I'm pulling your leg. On the other hand if I tell you that to let no day pass without discussing goodness and all the other subjects about which you hear me talking and examining both myself and others is really the very

best thing that a man can do, and that life without this sort of examination is not worth living, you will be even less inclined to believe me. Nevertheless that is how it is, gentlemen, as I maintain, though it is not easy to convince you of it.

Some governments today seem more sympathetic to the spirit of Plato than that of Socrates: they want to control outcomes by controlling expression. The future of free speech is uncertain. If we recognize free speech's centrality to democracy then perhaps we will be more ready to dig our heels in at a certain point and not yield to pressure that would have us censor ourselves for fear of offending someone. In Britain the government's recent readiness to sacrifice free speech for the sake of other values such as security and religious sensitivity to offence is a worrying sign. It is an indication that the arguments about the value of extensive free speech for the legitimacy of democracy as well as for individual freedom have not carried much weight with those in power. But it is easy to be persuaded by the rhetoric of free expression that all curbs on this freedom are morally objectionable, which they aren't. Sometimes we do need to give greater weight to other considerations, to rank another value higher. For example, some kinds of extreme pornography should not be allowed to shelter under the umbrella of free speech. We must be clear, though, why, for example, child protection is of greater importance than free speech, and we must also be clear about where we want to draw a line and why.

Free speech is not simply an issue for ivory tower abstract discussion. On the contrary, as Helena Kennedy has written:

> Free speech is one of the core values in a democracy and it should be championed with a vengeance.

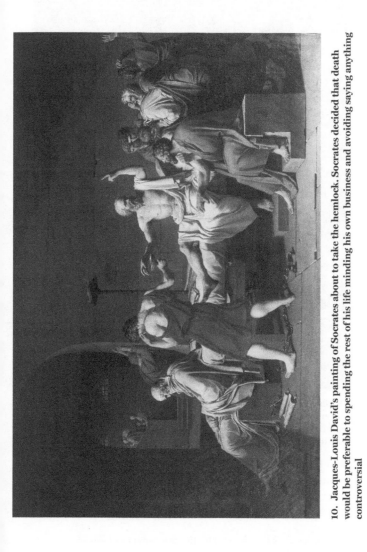

10. Jacques-Louis David's painting of Socrates about to take the hemlock. Socrates decided that death would be preferable to spending the rest of his life minding his own business and avoiding saying anything controversial

11. Shortly after coming to power in 1933 the Nazis burnt books by 'degenerate' authors in public bonfires in cities across Germany. Writers whose works were burnt included Kafka, Marx, Freud, Einstein, Mann, Rilke, and Hemingway

Why is it so central to democracy? One view, which I have already mentioned, endorsed by Ronald Dworkin, is that no democratic government can claim legitimacy unless it allows its citizens freely to debate whatever they wish to debate.

Free speech is a condition of legitimate government. Laws and policies are not legitimate unless they have been adopted through a democratic process, and a process is not democratic if government has prevented anyone from expressing his convictions about what those laws and policies should be.

At the very least voters in a democratic society need access to a wide range of views if they are to make informed choices. This is a theme I have emphasized throughout this book.

The Internet democratizes communication, at least for those who can afford to connect to it. More people than ever before can speak to each other and be heard across the globe. When those who speak out against oppression are silenced, news about this silencing is far more likely to escape to the rest of the world than has ever been the case. Toleration of free speech may in the future be the result of the practical difficulty of silencing so many voices with so many ways around mainstream media rather than of any principled decision. But there is no inevitability about this result. And some states are working very hard to control their citizens' access to information from the Internet, using every technical device at their disposal.

In Ray Bradbury's dystopian *Fahrenheit 451*, a novel in part inspired by the Nazi book burnings of the 1930s, the central character's job is destroying books. The title refers to the temperature at which paper combusts. Getting rid of awkward thoughts simplifies life—in this imagined future anything that could interfere with mindless happiness is incinerated; anything that anyone finds offensive ends up in ashes. In the end the people are scarcely aware that they have lost anything. That is another possible future.

Free speech: some key dates

399BC	Socrates, charged with impiety and corrupting the Athenian youth says he'd rather die than give up expressing his views. He is condemned to death and drinks hemlock.
1633	Galileo's *Dialogue on the Two Great World Systems* is banned by Pope Urban VIII. Galileo's view that Earth revolves around the Sun proved correct.
1644	John Milton's *Areopagitica* is published. Milton defended unlicensed printing.
1689	John Locke's 'A Letter Concerning Toleration' is published. Locke argued for extensive religious toleration, though he did not extend this to atheists.
1791	First Amendment to the United States Constitution. This prohibits Congress from making laws which curtail freedom of speech.
1859	John Stuart Mill's *On Liberty* published. This contains the highly influential Chapter 2, which defends freedom of speech.
1919	Justice Oliver Wendell Holmes Jr. in the case *Schenk vs United States* coins the phrase 'clear and present danger' in relation to the circumstances in which free speech can be overridden.
1933	10 May: Nazis organize book burnings in many cities in Germany. Authors whose works were burned include Marx, Freud, Kafka, Hemingway.
1948	Universal Human Rights declared. These include a right to free speech.

1960   The *Lady Chatterley* trial in the United Kingdom investigates whether or not Lawrence's book is obscene. The verdict is that it can be published. This results in a far greater freedom of publication in the United Kingdom than ever before.

1977   In London *Gay News*'s editor Denis Lemon receives a fine and suspended sentence for the blasphemous publication of a poem which depicts Christ as a homosexual.

1989   Iran's Ayatollah Khomeini pronounces a *fatwa* against Salman Rushdie. His book *The Satanic Verses* was burned publicly in Bradford. The Japanese translator of the book is killed.

2000   Deborah Lipstadt and her publisher Penguin win landmark libel case against David Irving, who objected to her describing him as a Holocaust denier.

2004   Murder of Theo Van Gogh for the film *Submission*. Ayaan Hirsi Ali, who wrote the script is threatened.

2005   Danish newspaper *Jyllands-Posten* publishes twelve cartoons, most of which depict Muhammed. As a result there are violent protests in many countries.

References

Chapter 1

R. Dworkin, 'The Right to Ridicule', *New York Review of Books*, 53/5 (23 Mar. 2006).

T. M. Scanlon on 'Ethics Bites' podcast. This podcast and transcript are available from www.open2.net/ethicsbites/

A. Meiklejohn, 'Freedom of Speech', in P. Radcliff (ed.), *Limits of Liberty: Studies of Mill's* On Liberty (Belmont, CA: Wadsworth, 1966), pp. 19–26.

J. S. Mill, *On Liberty* (1859; Harmondsworth: Penguin, 1974).

Oliver Wendell Holmes Jr's observation that freedom of speech should not include the freedom to shout 'Fire!' in a crowded theatre is quoted in G. Edward White, *Oliver Wendell Holmes Jr* (Oxford: Oxford University Press, 2006). White points out that Holmes wasn't completely consistent in his application of the 'clear and present danger' criterion in subsequent cases.

Holmes's declaration that special circumstances justified a special restriction on freedom is quoted in '*Schenck v. United States* 249. U.S. 47 (1919)', in R. A. Posner (ed.), *The Essential Holmes* (Chicago, IL: University of Chicago Press, 1992), p. 315.

The 'best test of truth' quotation is from G. Edward White, *Oliver Wendell Holmes Jr* (Oxford: Oxford University Press, 2006), p. 110.

Sue Hemming from the CPS is quoted on the BBC website at: http://news.bbc.co.uk/2/hi/uk_news/6235279.stm

Chapter 2

Quotations from J. S. Mill, *On Liberty*, are from the Penguin edition (Harmondsworth, 1974), pp. 123, 76, 105, and 119.

The passage that David Irving objected to can be found in D. Lipstadt, *Denying the Holocaust: The Growing Assault on Truth and Memory* (Harmondsworth: Penguin, 1994), p. 181.

The judge's comments can be found in D. Lipstadt, *History on Trial: My Day in Court with David Irving* (New York: HarperCollins, 2006), pp. 274–5.

The Calgary quotation is from Lipstadt, *History on Trial*, p. 84.

The Alan Dershowitz quotation is from Lipstadt, *History on Trial*, p. 304.

The 'that would look great on your CV' quotation is from R. Dworkin, 'The Right to Ridicule', *New York Review of Books*, 53/5 (23 Mar. 2006), p. 281.

Chapter 3

P. Tatchell, *New Humanist*, 117/3 (Autumn 2002).

Stewart Lee, podcast *Thought for the World*, 23 February 2007, www.thoughtfortheworld.org/media/2007-02-11_stewartlee.mp3

L. Appignanesi (ed.), *Free Expression is No Offence* (London: Penguin in association with PEN, 2005), contains the quotations from Rowan Atkinson ('The Opposition's Case', p. 60), Philip Henscher ('Free Speech Responsibly', pp. 76–7), and G. K. Bhatti ('A Letter', p. 28).

O. Kamm, 'New Labour: The Tyranny of Moderation', *Index on Censorship*, 36/2 (2007), 84.

R. A. Posner, 'The Speech Market and the Legacy of *Schenck*', in L. C. Bollinger and G. R. Stone (eds.), *Eternally Vigilant: Free Speech in the Modern Era* (London: University of Chicago Press, 2002), p. 136.

Ali's attack on Islamic teaching is from A. H. Ali, *Infidel: My Life* (London: The Free Press, 2007), p. 314.

Further citations from Ali are from A. H. Ali, *The Caged Virgin: A Muslim Woman's Cry for Reason* (New York: Free Press, 2006), pp. 157, 141, and 154.

K. Malik, 'Don't Incite Censorship', *Index on Censorship*, 36/2 (2007), 81.

Chapter 4

For the controversial definition of pornography, see C. MacKinnon,
Only Words (London: HarperCollins, 1995), p. 87.

F. Schauer, *Free Speech: A Philosophical Enquiry* (Cambridge:
Cambridge University Press, 1982), p. 181.

The MacKinnon quotation concerning pornography as a free speech
issue can be found on p. x of *Only Words*, the 'desperate women'
quotation on p. 14, and 'living out' pornography on p. 13.

B. Williams (ed.), *Obscenity and Film Censorship: An Abridgement of
the Williams Report* (Cambridge: Cambridge University Press,
1981), p. 57.

The 'negative liberty' quotation is from R. Dworkin, 'Liberty and
Pornography', *New York Review of Books*, 38/4 (15 Aug. 1991).

'Liberals defend pornography' is from R. Dworkin, 'Women and
Pornography', *New York Review of Books*, 40/17 (21 Oct. 1993).

Mapplethorpe is cited in A. Mahon, *Eroticism and Art* (Oxford:
Oxford University Press, 2005), pp. 230–1.

Chapter 5

R. A. Posner, 'The Speech Market and the Legacy of *Schenck*', in L. C.
Bollinger and G. R. Stone (eds.), *Eternally Vigilant: Free Speech in
the Modern Era* (London: University of Chicago Press, 2002),
p. 150.

C. R. Sunstein, 'The Future of Free Speech', in L. C. Bollinger and G. R.
Stone (eds.), *Eternally Vigilant: Free Speech in the Modern Era*
(London: University of Chicago Press, 2002), p. 285.

Conclusion

The Socrates quotation is from Plato, *The Apology* 37e–38b, *Last Days
of Socrates*, rev. H. Tarrant (London: Penguin, 2003).

H. Kennedy, 'Postscript', in L. Appignanesi (ed.), *Free Expression is No
Offence* (London: Penguin in association with PEN, 2005), p. 246.

R. Dworkin, 'The Right to Ridicule', *New York Review of Books*, 53/5
(23 Mar. 2006).

Further reading

There are up-to-date links to Internet resources and suggested further reading at www.vsi-free-speech.com.

General books on free speech

The A–Z of Free Expression (London: Index on Censorship, 2003) includes extracts from writers on many different aspects of this subject. It also includes Ronald Dworkin's essay 'A New Map of Censorship'.

Lisa Appignanesi (ed.), *Free Expression is No Offence* (London: Penguin in association with PEN, 2005) is a very interesting collection of essays by writers defending free speech, stimulated by proposed laws on religious hatred in the UK. Contributors include Salman Rushdie, Rowan Atkinson, Philip Hensher, Philip Pullman, Michael Ignatief, Hanif Kureishi, Adam Smith, and Helena Kennedy. The book was published in association with PEN, which is an organization that champions freedom of expression worldwide, particularly for writers and artists. Further details about PEN are available from www.englishpen.org.

Eric Barendt, *Freedom of Speech*, 2nd edn. (Oxford: Oxford University Press, 2005). Written by a professor of media law, this book addresses legal and constitutional issues, but also draws on political and philosophical thought. This is probably the most comprehensive treatment of the topic currently available. It provides a more detailed account of most of the topics raised in this book (and many others besides), together with a discussion of the key legal cases.

Lee C. Bollinger and Geoffrey R. Stone (eds.), *Eternally Vigilant: Free Speech in the Modern Era* (Chicago: University of Chicago Press, 2002) is an excellent anthology on First Amendment issues, and includes essays by Stanley Fish, Richard A. Posner, Frederick Schauer, Cass R. Sunstein, and others.

Alan Haworth, *Free Speech* (London: Routledge, 1998) is a wide-ranging philosophical treatment of free speech.

John Durham Peters, *Courting the Abyss: Free Speech and the Liberal Tradition* (Chicago: University of Chicago Press, 2005) is a recent exploration of the Anglo-American free speech tradition.

T. M. Scanlon, *The Difficulty of Tolerance: Essays in Political Philosophy* (Cambridge: Cambridge University Press, 2003) includes several important articles on free speech.

Frederick Schauer, *Free Speech: A Philosophical Enquiry* (Cambridge: Cambridge University Press, 1982) is a clear, well-argued treatment of the topic that is still relevant to present-day debates.

Index

Visit the
VERY SHORT
INTRODUCTIONS
Web site

www.oup.co.uk/vsi

➤ **Information** about all published titles

➤ News of **forthcoming books**

➤ **Extracts** from the books, including titles
  not yet published

➤ **Reviews** and views

➤ **Links** to other **web sites** and main
  OUP web page

➤ Information about **VSIs in translation**

➤ **Contact** the editors

➤ **Order** other **VSIs** on-line